SCOTLAND'S NEW WRITING THEATRE

Traverse Theatre Company

Homers

by

Iain F MacLeod

Until the late 1960s it was commonplace
for orphans from the central belt of Scotland to be
boarded out with families in the Highlands and Islands.
These children were known as homers.

**First performed at the Traverse Theatre
Saturday 5 October 2002**

Cast in order of appearance

Alex   Alastair G Bruce
Mary   Mary Gapinski
homers from Glasgow. Fourteen

Calum   Iain Macrae
Catherine Ann   Annie Grace
parents of the family Alex and Mary
are sent to stay with

Micheal   Alasdair Macrae
their son

Miss Scott   Iain Macrae
the schoolteacher

Christopher the Ceard   Stephen Docherty
schoolboy from a family of travellers

Minister   Alasdair Macrae
the village minister; devoted Elvis fan

Mrs Gunn   Stephen Docherty
Miss Scott's sidekick

Andrena   Annie Grace
a Lewis woman with unusual serving
suggestions for Hebridean delicacies

Alasdair Mor   Iain Macrae
her lamb-castrating husband

Priest   Stephen Docherty
a Glaswegian-born hermit ex-priest

Whaler   Annie Grace
a whaler (now retired)

Pig   Stephen Docherty
a butcher whom Alex goes to
for his apprenticeship in Glagsow

Shooey   Alasdair Macrae
butcher's apprentice

All other parts played by members of the company:
residents of Stornaway, schoolchildren, movie stars, etc.

Creative Team

Director	Philip Howard
Designer	Mary Robson
Lighting Designer	Renny Robertson
Composer	Anna Mhoireach
Sound Designer	Quee MacAuthur
Voice and Dialect Coach	Ros Steen
Assistant Director	Lorne Campbell
Stage Manager	Gavin Harding
Deputy Stage Manager	Mickey Graham
Assistant Stage Manager	Gemma Smith
Wardrobe Supervisor	Lynn Ferguson
Wardrobe Assistant	Stephanie Thorburn
Deputy Electrician	Maria Bechaalani
Carpenter	Hal Jones
Musicians	Quee MacAuthur
	Iain F MacLeod
	Anna Mhoireach

TRAVERSE THEATRE

powerhouse of new writing DAILY TELEGRAPH

Artistic Director Philip Howard

The Traverse is Scotland's new writing theatre. Founded in 1963 by a group of maverick artists and enthusiasts, it began as an imaginative attempt to capture the spirit of adventure and experimentation of the Edinburgh Festival all year round. Throughout the decades, the Traverse has evolved and grown in artistic output and ambition. It has refined its mission by strengthening its commitment to producing new plays by Scottish and international playwrights and actively nurturing them throughout their careers. Traverse productions have been seen world wide and tour regularly throughout the UK and overseas.

The Traverse has produced over 600 new plays in its lifetime and, through a spirit of innovation and risk-taking, has launched the careers of many of the country's best known writers. From, among others, Stanley Eveling in the 1960s, John Byrne in the 1970s, Liz Lochhead in the 1980s, to David Greig and David Harrower in the 1990s, the Traverse is unique in Scotland in its dedication to new writing. It fulfils the crucial role of providing the infrastructure, professional professional support and expertise to ensure the development of a dynamic theatre culture for Scotland.

The Traverse's activities encompass every aspect of playwriting and production, providing and facilitating play reading panels, script development workshops, rehearsed readings, public playwriting workshops, writers groups, a public playwrights platform, The Monday Lizard, discussions and special events. The Traverse's work with young people is of supreme importance and takes the form of encouraging playwriting through its flagship education project, Class Act, as well as the Traverse Young Writers Group.

Edinburgh's Traverse Theatre is a mini-festival in itself THE TIMES

From its conception in the 1960s, the Traverse has remained a pivotal venue during the Edinburgh Festival. It receives enormous critical and audience acclaim for its programming, as well as regularly winning awards. The year 2001 was no different with the Traverse being awarded two Scotsman Fringe Firsts and two Herald Angels for its own productions *Gagarin Way* and *Wiping My Mother's Arse* and a Herald Archangel for overall artistic excellence.

For further information on the Traverse Theatre's activities and history, an online resource is available at www.virtualtraverse.com. To find out about ways to support the Traverse, please contact Jayne Gross, Development Manager, on 0131 228 3223.

www.traverse.co.uk • www.virtualtraverse.co.uk

TEN YEARS OF THE TRAVERSE'S
HIGHLAND TOUR & WRITERS PROJECT

1993   LOOSE ENDS by Stuart Hepburn
1994   GRACE IN AMERICA by Antoine Ò Flatharta
1995   KNIVES IN HENS by David Harrower
1996   FAITH HEALER by Brian Friel
1997   LAZYBED by Iain Crichton Smith
1998   HERITAGE by Nicola McCartney
1999   HIGHLAND SHORTS: seven short plays
        by Highland & Island writers
2000   AMONG UNBROKEN HEARTS by Henry Adam
2001   THE BALLAD OF CRAZY PAOLA by Arne Sierens
        in a version by Stephen Greenhorn
2002   **HOMERS by Iain F MacLeod**
2003   OUTLYING ISLANDS by David Greig

The Traverse's work in the Highlands & Islands over the past decade has been a unique combination of touring production – usually a brand new play – and accompanying playwriting workshops. The aim always has been to provide Highland audiences with a rich mix of new drama while also developing the work of Highland playwrights – and of course ultimately to combine the two, as in the case of Homers. One of the benefits of this system is to ensure that writing development does not exist in a cocoon, away from the reality of production and the demands of audiences. And by mixing plays by writers from, say, Belgium, Edinburgh and Ness on the Isle of Lewis, the diet remains varied.

The Traverse has long recognised that, to make any impact at all on audiences and fledgling playwrights, a long-term commitment is essential, and so for many years we have been the only theatre company in Scotland to tour the North of Scotland on an annual basis, backed up by frequent visits to Eden Court Theatre, Inverness, with larger-scale work.

With thanks to the Scottish Arts Council and HI Arts for consistent support; and the playwrights who have led the Writers Project: Tom McGrath, David Harrower, Nicola McCartney, Henry Adam, and the late Iain Crichton Smith.

Philip Howard
Traverse Theatre
October 2002

COMPANY BIOGRAPHIES

Alastair G Bruce (*Alex*)   Trained: Royal Scottish Academy of Music and Drama in Glasgow. Theatre work includes: PASSING PLACES, ION, THE COUNTRY WIFE, SIX CHARACTERS IN SEARCH OF AN AUTHOR, THE SPECULATOR (RSAMD), JACK AND THE BEANSTALK (Adam Smith); SLEEPING BEAUTY (Brunton), JUST ONE MORE DANCE (Tramway), GRAND CENTRAL ADIEU (Gate Theatre) and Aladdin in the King's Theatre Glasgow (Dec 2002). Radio, Film, TV includes: Corum in URBAN GOTHIC: NECROMANCE (CH5), Mark True in THE REAL TARTAN ARMY (BBC2), Revolutionary in AMONG TIGERS WILD (Independent Short), Presenter for HIGHER STILL: LOCAL GOVERNMENT (BBC Education) and Scott MacLean in MOVING ON (BBC R4)

Lorne Campbell (Assistant Director)   Lorne's assistant directorship at the Traverse is funded by Channel 4 Theatre Director Scheme. Before joining the Traverse he ran Forge Theatre Company for four years. His directing credits include MADIEN, THE CHEVIOT, THE STAG AND THE BLACK BLACK OIL, THE CHAIRS, THE DUMB WAITER, COMEDY OF ERRORS, OLEANNA. Trained: MA at RSAMD, BA at Liverpool John Moores.

Stephen Docherty (*Priest, Christopher the Ceard, Mrs Gunn, Pig*) Theatre includes ANGELS IN AMERICA (Sheffield Crucible), BABYCAKES (Drill Hall, Traverse, Tron), A LITTLE OLDER (Hampstead Theatre, U.S. and European Tour), HOUSE AMONG THE STARS, GRAND MAGIC and SCHOOL FOR SCANDAL (Perth Rep Theatre), BREADMAKERS (Citizens Theatre/Mayfest), LION IN THE STREETS (Arches Theatre Glasgow), BODY AND SOUL (Caird Company London), and most recently THE PLAY O' THE WATHER at the Underbelly. Television work includes: THE ACID HOUSE (Channel Four), BUMPING THE ODDS (BBC); DOUBLE NOUGAT (BBC Scotland). Film work includes: MY NAME IS JOE (Parallax Film), ORPHANS (dir Peter Mullan, Parallax Films), POST MORTEM (US Feature).

Mary Gapinski (*Mary*)   Mary graduated from Strathclyde University in 1998 with a BA Community Arts and then worked as Depute Artistic Director for West Lothian Youth Theatre until October 2001. Theatre work includes: THE PLAY O' THE WATHER (Nutshell), DR KORCZACKS EXAMPLE (TAG Theatre), BOILING POINT (Inter-Act Theatre), JUST ONE MORE DANCE (Glasgow City Council), PINOCCHIO (Cumbernauld Theatre), LION IN THE STREETS (The Arches New Stage Directors), HEALTH AND SAFETY & SOUND SCAPES (The Arches Festival of New Theatre), HOW TO SAY GOODBYE (Clyde Unity Theatre).

Annie Grace (*Catherine Ann, Andrena, Whaler*) For Theatre collective @Highland THE ACCIDENTAL DEATH OF AN ACCORDIONIST (2001 & 2002), THE WEDDING. For Wildcat THE CELTIC STORY. For the BBC: THE GAMEKEEPER soundtrack. Previous projects include IRON HORSE, SCOTTISH WOMEN, FEMALE FACTORY (Netherlands, Russia, Spain).

Philip Howard (Director) Philip trained at the Royal Court Theatre, London, on the Regional Theatre Young Director Scheme from 1988-90. He was Associate Director at the Traverse from 1993-96, and has been Artistic Director since 1996. Productions for the Traverse include: OUTLYING ISLANDS, THE BALLAD OF CRAZY PAOLA, WIPING MY MOTHER'S ARSE, THE TRESTLE AT POPE LICK CREEK, SHETLAND SAGA, SOLEMN MASS FOR A FULL MOON IN SUMMER (with Ros Steen), HIGHLAND SHORTS, THE SPECULATOR, HERITAGE (1998 & 2001), KILL THE OLD TORTURE THEIR YOUNG, THE CHIC NERDS, LAZYBED, WORMWOOD, FAITH HEALER, THE ARCHITECT, KNIVES IN HENS (also The Bush Theatre), EUROPE, BROTHERS OF THUNDER, LOOSE ENDS. Philip's other theatre includes HIPPOLYTUS (Arts Theatre Cambridge), ENTERTAINING MR SLOANE (Royal, Northampton) and SOMETHING ABOUT US (Lyric Hammersmith Studio).

Iain F MacLeod (Writer) For the Traverse: ALEXANDER SALAMANDER (Highland Shorts), CLIFF DANCING (National Gaelic Youth Theatre), SALVAGE (TOSG Theatre Company). His writing for TV includes MACHAIR for which he was also series editor. TV directing experience includes THE FAMILY (STV), MY BOY, THE MELBOST BARD – MURDO MACFARLANE (Best Arts Documentary, Celtic Film and TV Festival 2001), TACSI SERIES 5 (BBC SCOTLAND, BAFTA award for best arts programme, Best Entertainment Programme, Celtic Film and TV Festival), COLOURS (Best cinematography, Australian Industry Awards), CLEAS (STV/TNG), FROM TANGUSDALE TO TONGA, EXPERIMENTAL SCOTTISH ARTISTS (BBC), THERE YOU ARE/SIN THU FHEIN (STV). Iain has also released three albums with the Anna Murray Band.

Alasdair Macrae (*(Micheal, Minister, Shooey*) Trained at Longside College, Glasgow. His theatre credits include: THE BIG PICNIC (Promenade Productions), SABINA! (New Stage Theatre), PARAPHERNALIA, RAMP! THE RISE AND FALL OF EVEL KNIEVEL (Dougmax Productions), Berkoff's GREEK! (STG) BULL BALLET (Mischief La-Bas), THE STREET (Prime Productions), OUR BAD MAGNET (Tron theatre/Borderline co-production), PETER PAN

(Perth Rep), JACOBITES!, PUSS IN BOOTS, THE ANCIENT EGYPTIANS (Hopscotch), A REALLY BIG DOG (Arches). Film and TV; TEMPORARILY YOURS (Lorraine McGowan), FOOL'S GOLD: MAXIMUM MISCHIEF (BBC), THE IMPORTANT PARTS OF A TRUE STORY (Cineworks), FLAT (D&M Pictures). Alasdair also works extensively with Glasgow-based walkabout theatre group MISCHIEF, La-Bas, manifesting as everything from the ELVIS PRESLEY CLEANING CO. to THE LAIRD OF CALLYBREW. In his spare time he plays fiddle and bass with ceilidh bands The Oatcakes and The Tattie Howkers.

Quee MacArthur (Sound Designer)   Quee has recorded soundscores for Theatre, Dance, TV and Film and toured with Scottish bands Mouth Music, Sola and the Anna Murray Band. He is currently playing bass with Shooglenifty, Sunhoney and Finlay MacDonald. His compositions and recordings include: AN TEAGHLACH (TGSC), MEDEA and TIS A PITY SHE'S A WHORE (Theatre Babel), MO BHALACH (short film dir: Iain F MacLeod), ISLAND (HTV), UNSPOKEN and DECEPTION (X Factor), RED (Bolierhouse), Titles for NOCHT AN CHATALL, TRANSITIONS (soundtrack collaboration with Donald Shaw, James MacKintosh and James Grant).

Iain Macrae (*Calum, Miss Scott, Alasdair Mor*)   Trained: Mountview Theatre School, London. For the Traverse: TRESTLE AT POPE LICK CREEK, HIGHLAND SHORTS, HERITAGE, LAZYBED, PASSING PLACES. Other theatre includes: DEATH AND THE MAIDEN (Forge/York Theatre Royal), AN CLO MOR (Theatre Highland), BEGIN AGAIN (K+C), PHAEDRA'S LOVE (Ghostown), THE AIPPLE TREE (Dràma na h-Alba), SACRED GROUND (Watford Palace). Television includes: CROWDIE AND CREAM, KILLING OF THE RED FOX, INTERROGATION OF A HIGHLAND LASS, DWELLY, RAN DAN, YEAR OF THE PRINCE and DE-A-NIS? for the BBC; MACHAIR (STV), CIORSTAIDH (STV/Grampian). Voice for numerous TV cartoons. Radio includes: 'P' DIVISION, DESPERATE JOURNEY, THE LETTER, NORTHERN TRAWL (BBC). Film includes; THE GIFT, MAIRI MHOR (BBC), AS AN EILEAN (C4). Short films include: THE FLAT (only if in IFM's – D+M Productions); BEFORE WINTER WINDS, DATHAN (BBC).

Anna Mhoireach (Composer)   For the Traverse: LAZYBED. SCOTTISH WOMEN (Celtic Connections), FLAT (D + M Pictures), CROWDIE AND CREAM, DOTAMAN (BBC), TACSI (Eolas for BBC). Anna has recorded three solo albums, OUT OF THE BLUE; INTO INDIGO; TRI NITHEAN (KLR), and appeared on numerous compilations.

Ros Steen (Voice and Dialect Coach)   Trained at RSAMD: For the Traverse: OUTLYING ISLANDS, THE BALLAD OF CRAZY PAOLA, THE TRESTLE AT POPE LICK CREEK, HERITAGE, AMONG UNBROKEN HEARTS, SHETLAND SAGA, SOLEMN MASS FOR A FULL MOON IN SUMMER (as co-director), KING OF THE FIELDS, HIGHLAND SHORTS, LAZYBED, KNIVES IN HENS, PASSING PLACES, and SHARP SHORTS. Recent theatre work includes: NIGHTFLIGHTS, MEASURE FOR MEASURE, DISCO PIGS (Dundee Rep), OBSERVE THE SONS OF ULSTER MARCHING TOWARDS THE SOMME, GLUE, OLEANNA (Citizen's Theatre), VARIETY (Grid Iron), CAVE DWELLERS (7:84), EXILES (Jervis Young Directors/Young Vic), PLAYBOY OF THE WESTERN WORLD, LOVERS (Royal Lyceum Theatre), OLEANNA (Theatre Informer), A.D. (Raindog); SUNSET SONG (Prime Productions), SINGLES NIGHT, THE HANGING TREE (Lookout), CASANOVA (Suspect Culture), TRAVELS WITH MY AUNT (Brunton Theatre), BEUL nam BREUG (TOSG Theatar Gaidhlig), STROMA (TAG), TRAINSPOTTING (G&J Productions). Films include: SMALL LOVE, GREGORY'S TWO GIRLS, STELLA DOES TRICKS. TV includes 2000 ACRES OF SKY, MONARCH OF THE GLEN, HAMISH MACBETH and LOOKING AFTER JOJO.

Renny Robertson (Lighting Designer)   For the Traverse- FAITH HEALER, LAZYBED, WORMWOOD, CHIC NERDS, HERITAGE and TRESTLE AT POPE LICK CREEK. Other theatre includes BLOODED (Boilerhouse) and shows for Lung Has, Plan B, American Connexion and BLF.

Mary Robson (Designer)   Trained at Wimbledon School of Art. For the Traverse: LOOSE ENDS; GRACE IN AMERICA. Early work includes: designer for Fir Chlis, the first Scottish Gaelic professional theatre company; Tutor for six Drama Naiseanta n'Alba's summer schools. Recent theatre work includes WISE GUYS (Red Ladder/Contact Theatre). Mary has worked in the emergent field of arts in health for over ten years and is currently Project Director of Common Knowledge, the arts in health initiative of the Tyne and Wear Health Action Zone. She has worked on numerous creative projects with communities in a variety of settings both here and abroad.

SPONSORSHIP

Sponsorship income enables the Traverse to commission and produce new plays and to offer audiences a diverse and exciting programme of events throughout the year.

We would like to thank the following companies for their support throughout the year:

CORPORATE ASSOCIATE SCHEME

**Scottish Life the PENSION company
United Distillers & Vintners
Laurence Smith & Son Wine Merchants
Willis Corroon Scotland Ltd
Wired Nomad
Nicholas Groves Raines – Architects
Baillie Gifford
KPMG
Alan Thienot Champagne
Bairds Fine and Country Wines
Communicate
VFACTO**

MAJOR SPONSORS

navyblue

**This theatre has the support of the
Pearson Playwright's Scheme sponsored by Pearson plc**

The Traverse Trivia Quiz in association with Tennents

**with thanks to: Navy Blue Design Consultants
and Stewarts, graphic designers and printers
for the Traverse**

**Arts & Business
for management and mentoring services**

**Purchase of the Traverse Box Office,
computer network and technical and training equipment
has been made possible with money
from The Scottish Arts Council National Lottery Fund**

**The Traverse Theatre's work would not be possible
without the support of**

**The Traverse receives financial assistance for its
educational and development work from**

Calouste Gulbenkian Foundation, Peggy Ramsay Foundation,
Binks Trust, The Bulldog Prinsep Theatrical Fund, Esmee Fairbairn Trust,
The Garfield Weston Foundation, Gordon Fraser Charitable Trust,
Paul Hamlyn Foundation, The Craignish Trust, Lindsay's Charitable
Trust, Tay Charitable Trust, Ernest Cook Trust, The Wellcome Trust,
Sir John Fisher Foundation, Hanns and Elizabeth Rausing Charitable
Trust, Equity Trust Fund, The Cross Trust, N Smith Charitable Trust,
Douglas Heath Eves Charitable Trust, Bill and Margaret Nicol
Charitable Trust and Emile Littler Foundation

Charity No. SC002368

For their generous help on
HOMERS
the Traverse thanks

BFL
Herbal Cigarettes kindly donated by
Honeyrose Products Ltd, Stowmarket
George Allan, Oatridge Agricultural College
and everyone who kindly assisted
in the making of this production.

Sets, props and costumes for HOMERS
created by Traverse Workshops
(funded by the National Lottery)

Scottish
Arts Council
LOTTERY FUNDED

production photography by Douglas Robertson
print photography by Euan Myles

For their continued generous support
of Traverse productions the Traverse thanks

Habitat

Marks and Spencer, Princes Street

Camerabase

BHS

TRAVERSE THEATRE - THE COMPANY

Gillian Adams	Second Chef
Louise Anderson	Marketing & Press Assistant
Paul Axford	Corporate Development Co-ordinator
Maria Bechaalani	Deputy Electrician
Lorne Campbell	Assistant Director
Stuart Cargill	Assistant Chef
Andy Catlin	Marketing Manager
David Connell	Finance Manager
Neil Coull	Literary Assistant
Andrew Coulton	Assistant Electrician
Eric Dickinson	Kitchen Assistant
Jude Durnan	Deputy Box Office Manager
Lynn Ferguson	Wardrobe Supervisor
Michael Fraser	Theatre Manager
David Freeburn	Box Office Manager
Riccardo Galgani	Pearson Playwright in Residence
Susie Gray	Press & Marketing Officer
Mike Griffiths	Administrative Director
Jayne Gross	Development Manager
Kellie Harris	Head Chef
Philip Howard	Artistic Director
Hal Jones	Carpenter
Kevin McCune	Acting Deputy Bar Café Manager
Lara McDonald	Administrative Assistant
Stewart McDonald	Acting Assistant Bar Café Manager
Chris McDougall	Technical Stage Manager
Catherine Macneil	Artistic Administrator
Heather Marshall	Class Act Assistant
Katherine Mendelsohn	International Literary Associate
Nick Millar	Production Manager
Kate Nelson	Monday Lizard Co-ordinator
Pauleen Rafferty	Finance & Personnel Assistant
Renny Robertson	Chief Electrician
Hannah Rye	Literary Development Officer
Roxana Silbert	Literary Director
Zoe Squair	Front of House Manager
Stephanie Thorburn	Wardrobe Assistant
Margaret Todd	Accounts Support
Isabel Wright	Associate Playwright

Also working for the Traverse

Ewan Anderson, Marianne Barr, Nancy Birch, Kenny Brodie, Leo Buckingham,
Yvonne Cameron, Paul Claydon, Annie Divine, Jenny Duttine, Mary Ellis, Vikki Graves,
Linda Gunn, Sinead Harvey, Peter Hawkings, Claire Hilditch, David Inverarity,
Stephen Kipanda, Brooke Laing, Kate Leiper, Jon Ley, Kirsten Lloyd, Amy Logan,
John Lyndon, Euan McDonald, Hollie McDonald, Paul Nowak, Clare Padgett,
Andrew Pratt, Jennifer Reader, Tim Siddons, Jennie Smith, Alistair Stott,
Mark Thomson, Joe Vernon, Andy Young

TRAVERSE THEATRE BOARD OF DIRECTORS

Stuart Hepburn (Chair), Kate Atkinson, Roy Campbell, Steven Cotton, Leslie Evans,
Geraldine Gammell, Robin Harper MSP, Christine Hamilton, John Stone,
Stuart Murray (Company Secretary), Keith Welch

HOMERS

Iain F MacLeod

2

Characters

ALEX *and* MARY. *They are both fourteen. Both are homers from Glasgow, and have been sent from a home to live with a family in the islands.*

CALUM MACNEIL. *He is the father of the family that Alex and Mary go to stay with.*

CATHERINE ANN. *She is the mother. Calum and Catherine Ann are roughly in their mid to late thirties.*

MICHEAL. *Calum and Catherine Ann's son. He is the same age as Alex and Mary.*

MISS SCOTT. *The schoolteacher.*

CHRISTOPHER THE CEARD. *A schoolkid who gets into a fight with Alex.*

MINISTER. *The village minister.*

MRS GUNN. *Miss Scott's sidekick. A gossipy god-fearing old lady.*

ANDRENA. *Has a fetish involving Hebridean delicacies. Alex gets involved with her.*

ALASDAIR MOR. *Andrena's lamb-castrating husband.*

PRIEST. *An idiosyncratic ex-Priest that Alex and Mary get to know. He is fairly young – could be anything from late twenties to mid thirties.*

WHALER. *A small part. Was once swallowed by a whale and spat out four days later. Whenever he goes out of doors now, it starts to rain.*

PIG. *A rough Glaswegian butcher who Alex goes to for his apprenticeship in Glasgow.*

SHOOEY. *Pig's stuttering Glaswegian apprentice. He is sixteen.*

The main cast members will double up for some of the smaller parts. The play is written for six actors.

Scene One

MARY and ALEX *are homers. It is nineteen sixty-seven and they are being taken from a home in Glasgow and being sent to a family in the islands. They are both fourteen. They stand on stage, facing the audience.*

The set is quite fluid, with various objects of furniture being placed to denote various locations, i.e. the house, the church, the school etc.

At the moment the stage where they stand is quite empty. The late-night noise of a ferry leaving a pier.

MARY. Warm milk water black metal sky night breath wind.

ALEX. The whine and scrape of metal and paint straining ropes and clanging portcullis gate gangplank.

MARY. Thin line of land slipping wake framed away.

ALEX. Window of the day a black sky square then red pink hot on sea.

MARY. Rolling floor rolling sea saw boat through horse maned waves.

ALEX. Slipped off land wide circled horizon straight angled course for somewhere.

MARY. Where.

ALEX. Going somewhere.

Unsure cold wet deck.

They spy one another.

Are you Mary?

MARY. I'm Mary. Are you Alex?

ALEX. Yes. They told me to look out for a Mary. Said we were going the same place. Told me to make friends.

MARY. Are you from a home?

ALEX. Yes. You?

MARY (*nods*). Did they tell you where you were going?

ALEX. A kind of holiday.

MARY. Me too.

Pause.

ALEX. It's . . . a big boat.

MARY. It's big.

ALEX. Pretty big.

MARY. Want something to eat? We could get out of the cold.
   I've got some money . . . look.

ALEX. Yes please.

Beat.

MARY. Night turns day turns light.

ALEX. A thin strip appears.

MARY. Wake up. Wake up.

   We're here.

The sound of a ferry coming in to berth.

ALEX. The ferry doors like a seagull opening its jet wings.

MARY. What are they telegraph poles pointing at the sky.

ALEX. A sea of strangers pushing through the black salt-
   flavoured air onto the shiny seal back pier.

MARY. Wake up. Wake up. We're here.

The stage fills with people milling. ALEX *and* MARY *are
off the ferry and stand on the pier.*

ALEX. What do we do now?

MARY. Don't know.

   CATHERINE ANN (*the mother*), CALUM (*the father*) *and*
   MICHEAL (*their son*), *come on. They are dressed in their*

Sunday best and are looking around for ALEX *and* MARY. *There is a general air of confusion and bustle.*

CATHERINE ANN. Faic thu iad? [*Can you see them?*]

CALUM. Nach bidh iad a' fuireach aig an walkway, mar as àbhaist? [*Don't they usually stand at the walkway?*]

CATHERINE ANN. Chan fhaic mi iad. [*I can't see them.*]

CALUM. Dìreach . . . gabh air do shocair. Alright, Cha bhith iad fad as. [*Just . . . take it easy. Alright. They won't be far off.*]

MICHEAL. Sin iad. Thall an sin. [*There they are. Over there.*]

The three of them make their way over to where ALEX *and* MARY *are standing, looking about lost. They all stand in silence for a moment before they are introduced.*

CALUM. Did you have . . . a good trip?

ALEX *and* MARY *nod.*

MARY. Are you here to meet us?

A pause as CALUM *and* CATHERINE ANN *look at one another.*

CALUM. Nach eil fios aca'? [*Don't they know?*]

CATHERINE ANN. Siuthad . . . can rudeigin. Say something. [*Just . . . say something.*]

Beat.

CALUM. My name's Calum. This is Catherine Ann.

We're your. New parents.

ALEX. Whit?

CALUM. What?

ALEX. Whit?

CALUM (*to* CATHERINE ANN). Dè?

. . . dè tha ag radh? [*What . . . what's he saying?*]

CATHERINE ANN. And this is Micheal. He'll be in your class in school.

MICHEAL *comes shyly forward.* CATHERINE ANN *gives him a gentle push.*

Go on shake his hand.

MICHEAL *does so. He gives a wee nod to* MARY.

CALUM. So you had a good trip. The ferry wasn't too rough?

CATHERINE ANN. You must be hungry . . . we've got a feed waiting for you.

MARY (*quietly*). Our new parents.

CATHERINE ANN. Well . . . we'll be looking after you from now. Micheal, you help them with their bags.

MICHEAL. I'm hungry.

CATHERINE ANN. Micheal. We'll eat soon.

MICHEAL. So what happened to your real parents?

He gets a quick clip around the ear.

CATHERINE ANN. Get the bags.

MICHEAL *picks up their two small hold-alls.*

Let's get you both warmed up.

Scene Two

Lights come up on ALEX *and* MARY*'s bedroom. There are two small beds side by side.* ALEX *and* MARY *lie in them.*

MARY. I'm stuffed.

Pause.

ALEX. Listen to the rain.

MARY. I've not seen rain like it. Cleaning everything.

A slash of lightning outside.

ALEX. Fireflies.

CALUM *comes in.*

CALUM. Now, there's not too many rules to the house. I'll just get them out straight away. You look as if you won't be too much trouble . . . but we've heard of . . . well . . . I think it's best we know what footing were on. All I'm saying is that if we tell you to do something, you have to do it. You don't complain. There's plenty of work to be doing around the house and you'll be called on to do it. Just remember, it keeps a roof over your heads.

Pause.

Alright. Oidhche mhath. [*Goodnight.*]

CALUM *leaves.* CATHERINE ANN *comes in.*

CATHERINE ANN. Are you both alright?

MARY/ALEX. Yes thank you.

CATHERINE ANN. Enough to eat.

MARY/ALEX. Yes thank you.

CATHERINE ANN. Well . . . I hope you get some sleep. Oidhche mhath.

MARY/ALEX. Goodnight.

She leaves. CALUM *is outside the room.*

CALUM. I thought I told you not to put them in the same room?

CATHERINE ANN. Where else do you propose I put them?

CALUM. But they're not properly brother and sister.

CATHERINE ANN. They are now, a Chalum.

CALUM *and* CATHERINE ANN *leave.* ALEX *and* MARY *are trying to take it all in.*

MARY. It's so quiet.

ALEX. So quiet I can't sleep.

MARY. So dark I can't sleep.

Pause.

I can feel my breath in my throat. They can probably hear me breathing from across the other end of the island.

Pause.

ALEX. They never mentioned anything about this. Thought they said it was a holiday.

MARY. Doesn't look much like a holiday. Surely they would have given everyone else in the home a holiday.

ALEX. Well, one or two of ours went away. (*Beat.*) They never came back.

Pause.

What do you think?

MARY. I'm scared.

ALEX. Are you?

MARY. No.

Yes.

What do you think of them?

ALEX. They seem alright. I don't think he likes me.

MARY. I think that's his way. He's religious.

Pause.

She's nice.

It might. You know. Be better. Than it was in the home.

ALEX. Do you think we should ask tomorrow how long we'll be here.

MARY. Don't know.

Pause.

Can I sleep beside you tonight?

Pause.

ALEX. Just tonight.

She gets up and goes to his bed.

Your feet are cold.

MARY. Just budge up. Don't be so soft.

They get settled.

How are we getting to school on Monday?

ALEX. Calum said Micheal would take us down and look after us.

MARY. Hope school is in English. Weird language they speak here.

ALEX. Hope they're not expecting us to speak it.

MARY. Well. We can't. Can we.

ALEX. Can't.

MARY. Thought they were Germans first of all. They sound like water going down a plug.

ALEX *smiles quietly. They listen to the rain again.*

ALEX. It's strange. Being on an island. Surrounded by nothing.

Scene Three

CALUM *comes on and starts to prepare himself for church, putting his tie on. He admires himself.*

MARY. Mr MacNeil . . . or dad we were told to call him from now on, would sit in the middle of the church preening like a peacock. He loved it, sucking on sweets and winking at people. He'd soon be wishing he'd laid off with the winking that day.

The family are in the church.

CALUM. We'll sit here.

ALEX *gets down on one knee and crosses himself as Catholics do before they enter the pew.* MARY *is about to do it.*

What . . . what are you doing . . . are you . . . Catholics?

ALEX. Yes . . . Well. I think so.

CALUM *cuffs* ALEX *on the ear.*

CALUM. Jesus Christ.

He drags ALEX *up by the scruff of the neck and sits him down.*

Just copy me. Don't do anything I don't do.

MARY. The Minister droned on like a bee, the heat was cloying inside the church.

MINISTER. Hurdle gurdle chumping Jehosephat lamb chops flibberty flibberty . . . Red sea flopperty flopperty gideon Methuslelah! (*He carries on under* MARY.) . . . Holy Moses Nebuchadnezzar durghal shlurp dens of lions! Holy men on poles in deserts all this talk of giant turtles . . . sheds of hams and jaffas two by two a big pot of lovely steaming mince. And in the final days a giant lobster will bring . . . peace to this world! Forbidden shellfish flip floppety big Arks stuffed to the gunnels . . . Jesus Christ!

MARY. We would all sit around lined up like potato plants in our pews listening to the Minister. Watching the grass waving outside. Alex fell asleep to the rustle of pan drops until, as if hypnotised, the word peace wakes him up.

MINISTER. Bring peace to this world . . .

MARY. Open google saucer eyes.

ALEX. Peace be with you.

Peace be with you.

He starts shaking everyone's hands.

Peace be with you.

MINISTER (*as part of his sermon*) / CALUM (*as a swear*). Jesus Christ . . . !

MARY. By the time they got home our father walked straight to the

CALUM. Whisky.

CATHERINE ANN. On Sunday?

CALUM. Where is it?

They've sent us. He's sent us the wrong ones. These (*He points.*) are Catholic.

CATHERINE ANN. I don't think it's too much of a problem. And don't call them these.

CALUM. Not a problem! I was a laughing stock at the church. Crossing himself whenever the Minister finished a prayer. Crossing himself!

CATHERINE ANN. We can hardly just pack them off again.

CALUM. These children will drain me dry. Of respect you hear. A man loses his respect he loses everything. Draining me like a sieve. Well I'll teach him a lesson. He won't make a fool of me again like that.

MARY. The drink started moving through his veins.
Cuchulainn's hero light above his head. That night he tore
the place up and gave Alex a leathering he wouldn't forget.

CALUM. Drop your trousers boy.

He starts to belt ALEX.

ALEX. Slaish!

And again another slaish.

Where's the holy water?

Slaish.

Everyone google eyed at the peace be with yous slaish.

CALUM. Little bastards I knew they were going to be trouble
the moment I laid eyes on them sucking me dry as if they
were eating a crab.

He finishes the whipping. CALUM *is out of breath*

Are you alright boy.

You alright?

ALEX *lies in a heap on the floor.*

Jesus, boy. I hardly touched you. Get up.

CALUM *goes over to him. Puts his hand on him gently.*
ALEX *shrugs it off.*

Right.

He grabs him by the scruff of the neck and throws him out.

ALEX *groans with pain.*

ALEX. I was sent out the back of the house with some chicken
bones and a bowl of water. Like a dog. Sniff sniff. Howl at
the moon.

Sore. Sore. Red line sting from jellyfish belt. Poor little
cuilean. What's that? (*Sniffs, pricks up ears, afraid.*)

Mouse. Luchag.

MARY (*quietly*). Alex.

ALEX *sits up.*

ALEX. I'm here.

MARY. Are you alright?

ALEX. I've got a sore arse.

MARY. Did he break anything?

ALEX (*checks*). No.

MARY. Bloody . . . bastard. I'll show him.

ALEX. Mary, you'll just get into trouble.

MARY. We'll get him back. Don't you worry.

We'll teach him a lesson.

CATHERINE ANN *comes out.*

CATHERINE ANN. Alex, bheil thu alright a ghraidh? [*Alex, are you alright?*]

ALEX. I guess.

CATHERINE ANN. Let me see. *(She looks.)* Och you'll be whole before you marry.

ALEX *smiles weakly. There is an awkward pause.*

'Se duine math a th'ann an Calum. Calum's a good man. Sometimes he maybe . . . bidh e ag ol, 's mathaid, just a little . . . uaireannan bidh e a' call an temper aige. Like anybody else .. . Ach 'se duine math a th'ann. [*Calum's a good man. Sometimes he maybe . . . he has a drink, maybe, just a little . . . and he can lose his temper. Like anybody else . . . but he's a good man.*]

Pause.

He's just been worried about the whole thing. It's worrying for us as well. So I'd ask you to forgive him. He'll soon settle down to the idea and everything will be fine.

ALEX/MARY. Yes mam.

CATHERINE ANN. Now, both of you get to bed. You've got a big day ahead of you tomorrow. Siuthad. [*On you go.*]

Scene Four

The first day MARY *and* ALEX *go to school with* MICHEAL. *They are in the classroom.*

MARY. The next day we went to school for the first time.

The school was made up of invisible lines which neither of us knew. You didn't want to cross or break them.

There were a few other homers in the class, keeping quiet. They had been there longer than us.

Everything about them made them stand out. Their accents. Their boniness. The look in their eyes.

ALEX. They kept quiet. Like little luchagan.

MARY. This didn't bode well for Alex. He was noisy. As noisy as a tractor.

Pause.

MICHEAL. The homers usually sit at the front.

MARY. Can we not sit beside you?

MICHEAL. No. Shut up. And Dad said that if you didn't behave I'd get mo mhì-shealbh . . . so shut up and keep quiet. Try not to look straight at Miss Scott. She gets cross eyes and doesn't like it. So shut up.

ALEX. You've already said that.

MARY. And don't tell me to shut up.

MICHEAL. I'll tell you to shut up if I want. Because if you don't do what I say I'll make life hard for you.

MARY. Mam said you're supposed to look after us.

MICHEAL. She's not your mother. And I don't know why they want you here either. I'm telling you, if you get me into any trouble . . . I'll kill you.

He hears MISS SCOTT *coming up the corridor.*

Here she comes. Sit down. Shut up.

MISS SCOTT *enters the room.*

MISS SCOTT. Gideon! Ephesians! Methuselah!

WHOLE CLASS. Gideon! Ephesians! Methuselah!

MISS SCOTT. We have another two joining us. Once again at an odd time of the year . . . but . . .

You. The new boarded out.

ALEX. Me?

MISS SCOTT. What's your name?

ALEX. . . . Alex . . .

MISS SCOTT. And you?

MARY. Mary.

MISS SCOTT. Hmm . . . don't like the look of you. Anyway. We'll carry on with our Gaelic lessons. You (*To* ALEX *and* MARY.) Stay quiet.

Now! Repeat after me!

The cat sat on the mat. Shuidh an cat air a' mhat!

CLASS. Shuidh an cat air a' mhat!

MISS SCOTT. My goat is in the field. Will you please wash its feet.

Tha an gobhar anns an achadh. Nach glan thu na casan aige, mas e do thoil e.

CLASS (*mumbling*). Tha an gobhar anns an achadh. Nach glan thu na casan aige, mas e do thoil e.

MISS SCOTT. Calum and Mòrag ARE sitting on the road.

Tha Calum is Mòrag NAN SUIDHE air an rathad!

CLASS (*mumbling*). Tha Calum is Mòrag nan suidhe air an rathad!

MISS SCOTT. My fishing boat is small. BUT! it is big enough to catch fish.

Tha am bàt-iasgaich agam beag, ACH FHATHAST! Tha e mòr gu leor airson iasgach!

CLASS (*mumbling*). Tha am bàt-iasgach agam beag, ach fhathast! Tha e mòr gu leor airson iasgach!

MARY *puts her hand up.*

MISS SCOTT. Dishcloths are often found . . . (*Snaps at MARY.*) what is it?

MARY. What's the Gaelic for cat. Miss.

MISS SCOTT. Eh?

MARY. Only we've got some cats at home and I was wondering what their name was.

MISS SCOTT. Well. It's . . . cat.

Pause.

MARY. Well . . . it's not as hard as I thought.

The class giggle.

MISS SCOTT. Shaddap! Foghnaidh siud. (*Sounds like 'Shut up! Phoney shit.'*) [*Shaddap! That's enough!*]

MARY *looks a bit shocked. Thinks the teacher is swearing.*

Siud siud. (*Sounds like shit 'shit.'*). [*That's it.*]

Seadh gu dearbh. (*Sounds like 'shag a giraffe.'*) [*Right.*]

Continuaigidh sinn. [*We'll continue.*]

ALEX *bursts out laughing.* MISS SCOTT *slams her hands on the desk.*

You! Boarded out! What's so funny.

ALEX. Nothing Miss.

She grabs ALEX *by the scruff of the neck and drags him over to the corner.*

MISS SCOTT. Stand in the corner. If I hear another bìog out of you I'll hang you upside down you little bleigeard seen your likes before need a good sglogitty giraffe shag leobag leobag . . . .

MARY. School was a misery. And this was how it went for a wee while. But I knew Alex would soon put his feet somewhere they didn't belong.

And that somewhere . . . was Christopher.

ALEX. Christopher was a ceard. The biggest ceard you ever saw. He was a great big ceard [*tinker*].

CHRISTOPHER *comes on. He flexes. He exercises.*

His family never threw things out and he had built a home-made gym behind his house.

He would lift fridges above his head. He made weights out of car rims and fenceposts.

He would stand for three hours punching a put – a pink fishing buoy. Until his fingers were like a packet of beef sausages.

CHRISTOPHER. Any bastard . . . ANY BASTARD . . . tries it on with me. They've got some trouble going. They'd better kill me first, better do me properly, or else . . .

ALEX. The worst thing was that his family, his brothers . . . were like Russian dolls. His mother put them out as regularly as a sheep. Although you would never say this out loud or . . .

CHRISTOPHER. What did you say?

ALEX. Nothing.

CHRISTOPHER. I heard you. I HERD you, you little boarded out SHIT. Think I'm FUCKING DEATH! CAN'T HERE!

MARY (*to* MICHEAL). Gonna help him!

MICHEAL. It's his own look-out.

He turns his back on it. CHRISTOPHER *is about to swing for* ALEX *when* MARY *stands between them.*

MARY. Morning Christopher, lovely day.

CHRISTOPHER (*he isn't used to talking to girls*). Ouh . . . well . . . today . . . shum . . . cah . . . ashoo . . . froob . . .

MARY. Ah now.

She takes a shinty caman off someone who is watching the fight and hits CHRISTOPHER *on the knee with it. His knee goes to the ground.*

ALEX. He didn't like that. He was swinging around like a windmill his knee back to front sheep leg and then he grabbed another caman from one of the younger lads.

Then . . . BRAG!

I was sent reeling. Wibbley wobbley wibbley wobbley and little explosions doodlebugs bounce about fireflies and a sound like a radio and electric storm dots in the head.

MARY. Bzzz bzzz.

ALEX. Hot flies. Lead bees.

MARY. You hurt him!

MARY *jumps on* CHRISTOPHER, *grabs the caman and starts pummeling him.*

CHRISTOPHER. Fag mi! Fag mi! (*Sounds like 'Fuck me! Fuck me!'*) [*Leave me alone! Leave me alone!*]

MARY *is shocked.*

MARY. I will not!

Gives him another few good whacks. She finishes, wipes her hands and goes over to ALEX.

Are you OK?

ALEX. My head. Sore.

MARY. Serves you right.

ALEX. You shouldn't have hit him. Ceard'll kill me. They say he eats greenflyspray.

MARY. He was about to kill you anyway.

ALEX. I'd have managed . . . well . . . thanks for your help.

MARY. No bother. That bloody Micheal. I'll do him the next time I see him.

Come on. Let's go for a walk.

ALEX. But we're supposed to go back into class.

MARY. I hate it. I hate it here. I'm not staying. You can stay. I'm not staying.

ALEX. They'll miss us. Miss Scott'll notice.

MARY. Bet they won't. They just look through you when they talk to you. Anyway, I don't want to learn any more of her stupid sentences. (*Impersonates her.*) My goat is in the field . . . .

ALEX. It might get better when we settle in a bit. We won't stick out so much.

MARY. Don't you hate it here?

Pause.

ALEX. Yes.

Pause.

MARY. Just . . . come on.

MARY *makes to go,* ALEX *is still undecided. Then . . . they both go.*

Scene Five

ALEX *and* MARY *are hanging about at the cliffs.*

MARY. Near our house were cliffs rising like pillars to Heaven out of the sea. The sea frothed like warm milk at the bottom trying to gouge at them. There were memory crosses dotted round which had to be moved inland more and more as the tops crumbled away.

This was where we hid. We made this ours.

ALEX *with his arms outstretched, standing at the edge.*

MARY. Get away from the side.

ALEX. Gog-gag. Chicken.

MARY. Don't go there. You're too close.

ALEX. Don't you feel like jumping. To see what it would be like.

Pause. Stretches his arms out.

Jesus on a hundred foot tall cross.

And then a swallow dive.

And then quiet. Lightness and air rushing at you and spinning like a wheel.

MARY. You're not brave enough to be a bird. Alex, get back from the side.

He moves back.

ALEX. Bet you I could make it down.

MARY. Yeah, yeah. What's with the acting tough.

Something catches his eye.

ALEX. What's that down there?

MARY. What?

ALEX. A body.

MARY. I can't see anything.

ALEX. You have to look closely. It's way down, looks like it's hanging onto the side of that flat rock.

MARY. Jesus, so it is.

ALEX. Who do you think it is?

MARY. The guy who went missing?

ALEX. Seamus Dubh.

They look at one another.

MARY. The guy who went missing?

We should go and get somebody.

ALEX. I'm going to climb down and get him.

ALEX *stands up.*

MARY. Don't be daft. You need a boat . . . the sea makes a mess of bodies. It'll be pretty horrible. You might not be able to lift him up, even. He might just fall apart.

ALEX. I'm going down. You be the cockatoo.

MARY. Why me. I'm always the cockatoo.

ALEX. You're the girl.

MARY. You're saying I can't manage it?

ALEX *stands on the edge. A man has appeared. He is called* PRIEST. *He watches* ALEX.

PRIEST. Get back.

PRIEST *is dressed in fairly shabby old black clothes. He speaks with a Glaswegian accent. He is an ex-priest, but has dropped out of things as much as he can. He lives in a wee driftwood hut he has built.*

ALEX. Eh?

PRIEST. Do you want to kill yourself? You're too close.

MARY. We're not doing anything here, mister.

PRIEST. Get away from the edge.

PRIEST is edging closer to him. Then he bundles into him and pulls him to the ground.

ALEX. Get off me mister!

They messily disentangle themselves.

PRIEST. Take it easy, boy. I've just saved you.

ALEX. I wasn't doing anything.

MARY. He wasn't doing anything mister.

PRIEST. I know when someone's going to jump when I see one.

ALEX. I was going to climb down.

Pause.

PRIEST. Down there?

PRIEST looks down. He bursts out laughing.

ALEX. What's so funny about that?

PRIEST stops laughing.

PRIEST. Wake up! You'd have killed yourself.

MARY. Tell him about the body.

PRIEST. Body?

MARY. There's a body at the bottom of the cliff.

ALEX looks at her – as if she has given away a secret she really shouldn't have.

PRIEST. A body. Well let's have a look.

He crawls to the edge. ALEX *and* MARY *hang back.*

Well well.

ALEX. See mister.

PRIEST. An oilskin.

ALEX (*deflated*). An oilskin.

PRIEST. I'll need a long fishing line to reach that beauty.

MARY (*to* ALEX). Told you.

PRIEST. Why so sad? It's good news eh.

ALEX. We thought it was Seamus Dubh.

PRIEST. Ahh. No. Who knows where Seamus is.

MARY. My mam thinks he's in Australia.

ALEX gives her a nudge.

PRIEST. Well, that may be. Nobody knows for sure where he's gone to. Did you know he had a wife out there for ten years. In Australia. As well as the one he had here. An amazing example of concurrency. Never sent a penny home, just kept the two wives going for ten years. Amazing. You'd think one was enough.

He introduces himself.

I'm Priest.

ALEX and MARY look nervous for a second.

PRIEST. What?

MARY. Our mam told us about you.

PRIEST. What'd she say? Tell you not to come near? Don't worry kids. All the bogeyman's into is sitting here and having a little chat with my two new friends. That and having a smoke.

He takes some roll-ups out, he has some already rolled in a tobacco tin. ALEX and MARY are reluctant at first. But slowly they sit beside him.

Want one? Home made.

They shake their heads, no.

MARY. What do you do?

PRIEST. Nothing.

I just kick back. Live like a monk. (*He lights his cigarette and takes a drag.*) Take in the air.

ALEX. You live up there?

PRIEST. Yeah.

ALEX. Don't you get bored?

PRIEST. No. I'm a man of leisure.

ALEX. Nothing ever happens here anyway.

PRIEST. Eh?

ALEX. Nothing ever happens here.

PRIEST. Nothing?

Things don't stop happening here.

The place is tired of things happening. A holy man stood here like you or I an age ago and the ground beneath him as nameless as a blanket. And then he started to name the islands and the places which spread beneath him like a robe. He had chosen his spot, closer to God, further from man. Then people started to come. Strangers. Gaels. Then he saw the longboats.

Pause.

ALEX. What did he do then . . . ?

PRIEST. Well . . . he shat his pants, didn't he. Bloody Vikings and all that.

Shat his bloody pants.

MARY. You used to be a Priest?

PRIEST. Hard to believe eh. And then I discovered the joys of Mary Jane. And the Mamas and the Papas.

The rest is history. Or rather . . . it isn't.

He pauses. Stubs out the end of his roll-up and gets up.

Time to go.

See you around. Don't go jumping off anywhere now.

PRIEST *leaves.*

ALEX (*to audience*). Our mother was interested in what we had been up to.

CATHERINE ANN. Haven't I told you never to go up there and near the lighthouse as well and you talked to that man you'll be the death of me with all the worry you cause us myself and your father both I take my eye off you for one minute and you end up in the company of that man not a person in the whole village knows what kind of man he is what he's running away from he boils mushrooms in his tea you know he's not normal and he's not proper company for young children and all that carry on about a body.

She takes a breath.

Well you won't be going up there again. I've got just the thing for you.

Scene Six

CATHERINE ANN *leaves the stage.* ALEX *has a brush and an old boiler suit thrown at him.* MARY *an apron.*

MARY. We got jobs . . .

ALEX. . . . to keep us out of trouble. For a penny a week I was to sweep up and tidy up and wash up the hall after the coories had been in. (*'Coories' are religious people.*) This week they were at high-doh. Something about films being shown.

MARY. I was to clear up their left-overs. They made an awful mess with all those scones.

ALEX. That was when I met Andrena first of all.

ALEX, *left alone to sweep the floor, gives a sweep here and a sweep there. He looks around, then starts to waltz with the brush.*

Your hair . . . it's beautiful tonight . . .

. . . don't tell your husband . . .

ANDRENA *comes in.*

ANDRENA. Hello Alex.

He stops, embarrassed.

Giving the place a good clean?

ALEX. Aye.

ANDRENA. You know, I think you'd be perfect. I need some help at home. You'd be paid handsomely. My father, you see, is just a bit too old and I need someone to do lifting for me. I need a young man, like yourself.

ALEX. Are you sure I can help you?

ANDRENA. I'll give you double what you get here.

ALEX. Well. That sounds fine.

ANDRENA *seems happy with this.*

ALEX. So.

So . . . what would you like me to lift?

ANDRENA. Oh now, don't worry about that just now. (ANDRENA *eyes up the buffet table. It is meant for the meeting.*) Have you eaten?

ALEX. Not yet.

ANDRENA. Good. Good. (*She pats the chair beside her.*) Come here.

ALEX. Is your father around?

ANDRENA. Who? Oh you mean Alasdair Mòr. He doesn't get out much.

ALEX (*stumbling*). Oh . . . hope that that's going whatever he's working on well for him.

ANDRENA. Hmm.

Pause.

Do you know women, Alex?

ALEX. I know a few. Well, there's a few girls in school I've talked to. Mary my sister. And my mother of course . . . Peigi across the road . . . old Ishbel in the shop . . .

ANDRENA. No, Alex. Do you know them? Do your loins . . . gird when you think of them?

ALEX. Loins gird?

ANDRENA. Come, come. You're a good-looking boy. You must feel a certain rising. Or have you never been so close to a real woman like me before.

She moves closer to him.

Don't be scared Alex. Have a scone.

She unveils a beautiful plate of scones. She moves even closer and gives him a kiss. ALEX's *eyes open in surprise.*

I want you to eat it off me.

ALEX. Um. Alright. Where exactly?

She bares her midriff.

I meant eh . . . you mean . . . here?

ANDRENA. Yes.

ALEX. You mean . . . really. Off you?

ANDRENA. Shut up, Alex.

ALEX. But there'll soon be people here.

ANDRENA. Shut up!

They begin, ANDRENA *directing proceedings. She is enjoying it.* ALEX *looks confused.* ALEX *hears a noise and stops. She quickly re-arranges herself.* MARY *comes back in.*

There you go . . . we'll leave the heavy lifting today.

ANDRENA *leaves. Pinches his bum on the way out.*

MARY. What was that about?

ALEX. Oh . . . nothing.

MARY. You smell funny. Buttery.

ALEX. Don't you have cups to clear up?

MARY. I've done all of that.

ALEX. Oh . . . well then!

ALEX *hears someone coming.*

The cailleachs are here! [*The old biddies are here!*]

He runs off. MARY *makes herself inconspicuous in a corner.*

The MINISTER, MISS SCOTT *and* MRS GUNN *come in. The* MINISTER *has a little bit of Elvis about him. Sometimes he does a little uh-huh-huh Elvis move, and he seems to be dressed in a sort of ministerial Elvis jump suit.*

MRS GUNN is MISS SCOTT'*s side-kick, although she's not shy of speaking her own mind now and again. Big hips. Big calfs. Passion killer tights. Big hat*

Sometimes MISS SCOTT *has a weird kind of Hebridean Tourette's syndrome where she shouts out strange words. People often mishear what she says and think she has said something else.*

MISS SCOTT. As you can see a' Mhinistear we've prepared some FLATFISH! food for the meeting.

MINISTER. Thank you very much. Lovely lovely.

ALEX *comes on.*

ALEX. Cup of tea a' Mhinistear before the meeting starts? Take the thirst off.

MISS SCOTT. What's that DWARF! boarded-out boy doing here.

MINISTER. Alex and Mary clean the hall.

Any of . . . he-hem . . . Andrena's scones as well Alex lovely.

ALEX *goes*

MRS GUNN. You know, I worry.

MISS SCOTT. We all do. About this influx of ruffians from Glasgow.

MRS GUNN. I worry the effect it will have on the place. I just don't know what we'll do with them.This influx. That's exactly what it is.

MISS SCOTT. And that one in particular. The father would rather sit in his barn than show those LEOBAGS! [*flounders!*] children the way to behave probably not a word of scripture passed over the linoleum of that house since the poor grandmother died and even then it was always in the family.

Intakes of breath.

MRS GUNN. Always in the family.

MISS SCOTT. In the family.

MRS GUNN. It's in the family. You're right there's always been problems in that family knock knock on the head thanks be to God, we've none of that in our own family well cousins should never marry cousins I always say and let me tell you . . .

ANDRENA *comes on.* MISS SCOTT *and* MRS GUNN *carry on muttering in the background.*

MINISTER. Andrena, thank you for coming.

ANDRENA. Of course a' Mhinistear.

MINISTER. And you seemed to have magicked up another spread of . . . biblical proportions. If I am allowed to say that!

ANDRENA. I'm never happier than when I have something in the oven.

MINISTER. And lovely it is too. Uh-huh-huh. (*A wee lip curl*).

(*Pointedly to the ladies.*) I'm sure I can rely on you all of course.

He turns to the crowd/audience.

Well. Now we're all here, I'd like remind you of the reason for this week's meeting. The Film Guild and their impending visit to the area.

MISS SCOTT. My feet are furry with overuse!

Pause.

MINISTER. Excuse me?

MISS SCOTT. I said . . . It's a great worry for all of us.

MINISTER. It is indeed. For eggsample . . . look at this.

He brings out a poster – Attack of the Fifty Foot Woman! A gasp from the virginal MISS SCOTT. *A gasp from* MRS GUNN. *An interested look from* ANDRENA.

I have mounted it. To keep it stiff. As an example!

MISS SCOTT. Herds of goats at the gates of Rome!

Pause.

MINISTER. Excuse me . . . ?

MISS SCOTT. I said . . . I've heard of its grave effects when it comes.

MINISTER. Ah yes . . . so, we must gird our loins. There are others who are (*Sniff.*) for it. Now I have a projector with me so that I can show you the kind of . . . heh-hem . . . FILTH . . . they'll be screening in our midst.

MRS GUNN. Next they'll be showing French films.

ANDRENA. Are they bad?

MRS GUNN. Terrible! And the French. Always eating and . . . having the sex.

ANDRENA. Really . . . ?

MRS GUNN. Yes. I have such a . . . recipe book. I sometimes read it with my husband to remind us of the level people will go down to. Dirty dirty.

ANDRENA. How awful. Are there photos?

MRS GUNN. Yes! Mountains of puffy chocolate balls! Fish soups! Juicy hams!

MISS SCOTT. FRENCH! Filthy TROCADEROS! Fornicating goat dancing hyenas!

MINISTER. Em . . .

ANDRENA (*breathless*). I think I would like to see these photos.

MRS GUNN. I'm happy to show them to you. Any time.

MISS SCOTT. Herds of Stornoway marags! [*Black puddings.*]

Pause

I've heard its effect has been marked.

Pause.

Elsewhere. I said.

MINISTER. Would you like a glass of water or anything Miss Scott?

MISS SCOTT. I'm fine Minister. Gog-gag! Totally fine.

MINISTER. You're sure now.

MISS SCOTT. A1. First class.

MINISTER. Right.

From the back, a wee voice pipes up.

MARY. Well. I think I'd like to see some of these films.

Everyone turns to look at her.

MINISTER. Mary, the adults are talking.

MARY. Other places have them and they don't seem to do any harm.

MINISTER. They don't do any harm? Look at Stornoway!

MRS GUNN (*overlapping*). Stornoway . . .

MARY. Maybe we should have a vote.

MINISTER. Mary. Come now.

MARY. Or maybe you're scared you're wrong.

MINISTER. Mary . . . a wise man once said . . . only fools rush in . . . I've looked at it from all angles. You can be sure I've made the right decision.

MARY. I like to make my own decisions.

MINISTER. You are a very cheeky young lady.

Alright! Let's have a vote then!

All that are for, put your hands up.

Half of the crowd put their hands up. Including MARY *and* ANDRENA.

All those against.

The other half put their hands up.

So . . . a draw. The vote is undecided. Therefore there will be no films . . .

ANDRENA. Alex hasn't voted yet.

ALEX *has been daydreaming. The whole attention of the room turns to him.*

ALEX. What?

MINISTER. Is Alex's vote valid?

ANDRENA. Of course it is!

Alex?

MINISTER. Remember to vote the right way now, Alex.

MARY *is nodding to him – yes . . .*

ALEX. I vote . . .

I vote . . . yes.

The audience lets its breath go. Some happy, some not so happy.

MINISTER (*points at the projector*). Can you people not see that this is a golden bollock!

MISS SCOTT. CALF! In the geenglish they say golden calf.

MINISTER. Well. It shall be smote like the instrument of sin it is . . . splintered and burning it shall be . . . A curse on it! It is the bicycle which will take you all on the path to damnation . . .

MRS GUNN. Bicycles of damnation!

MISS SCOTT. Burning bush!

MINISTER. This will not be the last of this!

MRS GUNN. I hope not! I mean! It won't! (*She composes herself.*) Mar sin leibh. [*Goodbye.*]

ANDRENA. Cheerie.

MISS SCOTT. Markaig thus my words! Turbot eating martian life!

MRS GUNN. The Minister has left the building.

The MINISTER, MISS SCOTT *and* MRS GUNN *leave.*

MARY. How exciting is that? They're going to show films here.

ALEX. Listen . . . I was thinking of heading off.

MARY. Eh? You're not leaving me by myself to do everything. I'm off to clean the kitchen. You'd better have this place tidied by the time I'm finished.

ALEX *and* ANDRENA *are alone.*

ANDRENA. All clear?

ALEX. Someone could come back at any minute.

ANDRENA. I think we're safe my little one. Get the ceann cropaig, will you.

ALEX. Ceann cropaig. Onions and oatmeal and cod roe stuffed in a cod's head.

He goes to get it. ANDRENA *lies down on a table.*

ANDRENA. You can start.

She makes him smear ceann cropaig on her stomach and eat it off her.

ALEX (*to audience*). Andrena . . . seemed to have a thing about food and sex. Particularly Hebridean. The food of course, I mean. She seemed to like me eating it off her while she shouted to God.

ANDRENA. Oh yes. Eat some more. Oh God!

ALEX. I'm full.

She grabs him by the hair.

ANDRENA. Eat!

Some nice country and western music starts. ALEX *looks up in surprise, but his attention is swiftly returned to the task in hand.*

ANDRENA. Tell me how bad I am.

ALEX. Well . . . you are. Bad.

ANDRENA (*shouts*). Tell me!

ALEX (*shouts*). You're bad! Very bad!

ANDRENA. Now. For pudding!

Cranachan!

Cranachan is cream and oatmeal and strawberries. ALEX *spreads it on and starts eating.*

ALEX. Cranachan would send her wild. It must have been all that oatmeal. I didn't like it. It would get stuck in my teeth.

ANDRENA. Shut up and eat!

While they are at it a man comes in and stares, looking in disbelief as ALEX *and* ANDRENA *disentangle themselves. It is* ALASDAIR MOR, ANDRENA*'s husband.* ALEX *doesn't know this however.*

ALEX (*mouth full of cranachan*). Mr Alasdair Mor. I was just going to ask if I could see your daughter. Take her out, I mean.

ALASDAIR MOR. She's not my daughter. She's my wife.

Pause.

ALEX. Oh. Shit.

MARY (*comes in*). I think someone's coming to lock up Alex . . . are you almost . . .

MARY *stops and takes in the scene in front of her . . .*

Oh . . . bollocks.

ALASDAIR MOR. Andrena . . . how could you. The ceann cropaig.

Turns to ALEX.

I'll kill you. I'll cut your balls off you bloody little ceard.

ALEX (ALASDAIR MOR *freezes for a moment*).
Unfortunately for me he had been castrating the lambs, so he had the necessary tools to hand. He could show me a world of pain. Elastics and tobacco knife and pliers.

ALASDAIR MOR unfreezes. Chases ALEX round the table. Finally catches him and holds him in a clinch while he tries to organise his elastics. ANDRENA tries to stop him.

ALASDAIR MOR. Shut up am bioch.

ANDRENA looks around and spots a big pot. Grabs it and hits him over the head with it. It has been used to cook ceann cropaig.

The pan falls off. ALASDAIR MOR stands dumbfounded. A cod's head on his head. Like a hat. He falls over.

MARY. But! It turned out he wasn't killed. Just concussed by the cod.

ALEX speaks while ALASDAIR MOR is carried off.

ALEX. He was never quite the same again though. She was put where all bad women were put, for a while. Then she came back and joined the church and got a job cooking for the Minister whose wife had run off with a merchant seaman with big biceps. Oh well. For them, the course of true love never did run smoothly.

I'll never touch ceann cropaig again.

MARY. What were you doing?

ALEX. Nothing.

MARY. I had to clean up the whole place, and wash the dishes and everything while you were messing about.

ALEX. I wasn't messing about.

MARY. You were messing about with Andrena.

ALEX. So. What's it to you.

MARY. I'll just do all your work for you while you carry on with that handbag of a woman.

ALEX. That's fine.

MARY. If I don't get to see these films because of you, you'll be wishing Alasdair Mor did get a hold of you with his elastics.

ALEX. Mary . . . I didn't mean to upset you.

MARY. It's just the dishes. And things.

ALEX. I promise I'll do them all the next time. I didn't mean you to do them all.

Pause.

Will you still let me go to the film with you.

MARY. I guess.

Only because there's no one else.

ALEX. Let's go and do something for mam, then she'll let us see the film for sure.

MARY. OK.

Scene Seven

*Behind a screen some of the cast act out a scene from a
suitable film/musical of the time. MARY is transfixed by it.
A dance scene starts and MARY dances around, is carried in
the air by burly men etc. She speaks as this is happening.*

MARY. As if I was looking out through a huge window and the
juice of the world coming through it to me, sights I could
barely have conjured up in my own mind if I had sat for a
year and a day. And that's where I would spend all my time
– as much time as I could anyway.

One day I'd have the Hound of the Baskervilles after me.
Next day I'd be Audrey Hepburn admired by all the men I
wafted past . . .

*The film starts to go wrong, something has happened to the
projector. The dance stops and MARY stands still,
wondering what is going on.*

VOICE FROM OFF-STAGE. Projector's broken. Film's over.

MARY. Aw. I don't believe it. It was nearly the end.

*She gets up and goes outside. Looks around for ALEX but
there's no sign of him. Everyone else has gone.*

*ALEX comes and sits down beside MARY. He is a little out
of breath and looks as if he has been up to something. He is
smiling.*

Where have you been.

ALEX. Nowhere.

MARY. The projector's broken. Everyone's gone home.

I've been waiting ages out here for you.

ALEX smiles to himself.

What are you smiling for?

ALEX. I'm just smiling.

MARY. Did you have anything to do with the projector?

ALEX. No.

MARY. You did. Where have you been then?

ALEX. You should have seen his face when he woke up . . . he
thought the whole thing was going to go up . . . the film
tacka tacka going mad like a wee snake . . .

MARY. For God's sake Alex . . .

ALEX. Well, he shouldn't fall asleep when he's supposed to be
working should he.

MARY. I don't believe you sometimes. You know I've wanted
to see that film for ages.

ALEX. You can see it some other time.

MARY. They won't be showing it here again. You're always
spoiling things.

ALEX. It's just a stupid film. I didn't like it anyway.

Pause.

You don't even ask me to come with you any more.

MARY. Because you never watch them properly. You're always
fidgeting or throwing things at people or trying to get in the
way on the screen.

They pretty much turn their backs on one another. MARY
smells something.

Do you smell something?

ALEX. No.

MARY. Smells like something's on fire.

She goes over to the hall and looks in the window.

There's a fire! It's on fire!

ALEX *runs over to look.*

ALEX. Oh Jesus.

MARY. What have you done!

ALEX. I didn't do anything.

The noise of the fire starts to build.

MARY. We have to put it out.

ALEX. Mary, no!

MARY. We have to!

ALEX. The fire's too big, we need to go and get somebody.

They hear a noise.

There's someone over there.

They run over to where the person is. Out of the shadows comes the MINISTER.

A' Mhinistear . . .

MARY. Fire! You have to help us. There's a fire!

MINISTER. Really? (*Quite chuffed with himself.*) There is a God . . . Well. If I was the kind of person to say "I told you so" this would be the perfect time to do it. But I'm not.

MARY. Are you gonnae help or no!

MINISTER. I'll be back soon.

The MINISTER *goes.*

MARY. I don't understand. So quickly flames moving. My head is sore. Broken wheels and cogs inside metal case whirr whirr. Smoke curling like a tree's branches. The tongues licking up the side of the hall until it starts leaping from one side to the other. And the walls on flame like a solid sheet of rain roaring the noise filling my ears and wanting to lie down.

ALEX. Come on, let's go.

MARY *isn't moving.*

(*Picks her up.*) Come on!

The noise gets louder and louder until it fills the room.
CALUM *and some other locals run in, so the stage is*
milling as they try and organise themselves.

CALUM. We need water!

Did anyone call the fire engine!

ALEX. The fire was like a mad dancer. A dervish crackling
and whipping fire drenched wood spars.

CALUM. Is there anyone in there?

Are Alex or Mary in there?

Everyone is too busy to answer.

Damn it. (*Shouts.*) We need more water! Hurry up!

The villagers try and organise themselves to fight the fire.
ALEX *watches.* MARY *isn't to be seen.*

ALEX. The fire was like a dog out of control now. Nothing
would stop it. That is, until the whale man appeared.

The WHALER *appears and surveys the fire.*

The Whaler lived behind the hall. He had hardly been
outside his house for ten years. Ever since a whale
swallowed him and spat him up four days later.

Pah pah pah.

Hair as white as milk. As white as the moon. Out he
plopped. Like a new born goat. Blinking.

He never ate fish again. And he was obsessed with the
weather. Whenever he left the house to get his groceries. A
pint of milk or some drench for the sheep . . . It rained. It
rained like rain you'd never seen before. Cartwheeling out
of the sky.

And that's what happened at the hall. No sooner had they
heard . . .

WHALER. Looks like rain.

ALEX. Than they had to run for cover from the downpour.

The sound of a torrential downpour suddenly starts up.

Noah's flood was like spray from a boat in comparison. The spars of the hall crackled and popped until, like magic, the fire was gone.

The villagers stand. Exhausted but happy. The sound of rain stops.

WHALER. I knew it. Rain. Bloody rain.

WHALER *leaves.* CALUM *sees* ALEX.

CALUM. There you are! I thought you were in there! Thank God . . . you're alright . . . (*He notices* MARY *isn't there.*) Where's Mary?

ALEX *(looks around)*. I . . . I don't know . . . I left her over there . . .

CALUM. Is she in there?

ALEX. No.

CALUM. Are you sure?

ALEX. Yes . . . yes . . . definitely. She must have run off somewhere. She was with me when you were trying to put the fire out.

CALUM. Causing us nothing but worry.

ALEX. But I think I might . . . .

CALUM. Dùin do chlab! [*Shut up!*]Mary's gone missing . . . we need people to help look for her.

Scene Eight

An empty moor. It is misty and dark. MARY *runs on, she is out of breath. She stops.*

MARY. Cold.

Cold mist white eye closing mist. Got to watch cliff edge empty crumbling lip down to buttermilk water.

Got to watch.

Who would care.

Look at this place. I wish I could just disappear.

What have I done.

Pause.

Maybe I should go back.

I don't . . . I don't recognise this place . . . .

Hello . . . .

She shouts.

Hello . . .

Louder.

Hello!

Through the mist we see a torch beam darting about. It is PRIEST. *We hear him getting closer.*

PRIEST. Who's that there?

His torch alights on her.

Is that you. Mary?

What are you doing here? You'll catch your death.

MARY. I got lost. There was a fire at the hall and I ran off.

PRIEST. A fire?

MARY. What are you doing out here?

PRIEST. I live just over there. I heard someone shouting. (MARY *shivers*.) You're freezing . . . here.

He hands her his jacket. She moves away from him until she realises what he is doing. Then slowly she takes the jacket.

My hut is just up here, you can wait there while I go and get your father.

MARY. I'm OK. If you just point me the direction I should go.

PRIEST. I can't do that. What if something happens to you.

Pause.

MARY. Maybe I don't want to go home.

I hate this place. I want to leave here.

PRIEST. Catching pneumonia out here isn't going to help you much then, is it.

MARY. I guess not.

What'll I say about running away. It might look as if I had something to do with the fire. I didn't. I tried to myself and Alex stop it. I didn't do anything. We didn't.

PRIEST. I believe you, Mary.

Pause.

MARY. You're kind.

From offstage they hear shouts. It is CALUM and ALEX looking for MARY.

CALUM. Mhàiri!

MARY *hears them.*

MARY. Over here!

CALUM *and* ALEX *come on stage.*

CALUM. Thank God.

ALEX *runs over to her and gives her a hug.* CALUM *is a little surprised when he sees* PRIEST *there.*

ALEX. Are you alright.

MARY. I'm fine.

ALEX. Why did you run off on me?

PRIEST. She just lost her bearings a little.

MARY. Scared by the fire.

CALUM. Are you cold.

MARY. A little.

CALUM *takes his own jacket off and replaces* PRIEST*'s with it.*

CALUM. Alex, you start back with Mary. I'll catch up in a second.

ALEX. Alright. (*He puts an arm round* MARY.) Come on. (*He mouths the words to her.*) I'm sorry. (*She gives him a small smile.* CALUM *is left with* PRIEST.)

CALUM. Not wise for someone to be wandering around here, up at the cliffs at night. Anything could happen.

PRIEST. Lucky we found her.

CALUM. Lucky we found her in time.

He half gives/half throws the jacket back to PRIEST.

We cut to ALEX *and* MARY *together, waiting.* MARY *is cold.*

ALEX. Sorry about the films and stuff.

MARY. It doesn't matter really. Does it. When you think about it.

ALEX. Well. Sorry.

MARY. Do you think Calum'll be long?

ALEX. He shouldn't.

You're freezing.

He goes over to her and puts his arms around her and they wrap up tight, holding one another. Their faces close.

MARY. I got scared.

ALEX *holds her tighter.*

Cut to CALUM *and* PRIEST.

CALUM. I've been seeing more of you lately. Couple of times she's mentioned she's run into you.

PRIEST. We're friendly.

CALUM. You know she's only sixteen?

ALEX *and* MARY *look up from their clinch.* MARY *strokes* ALEX*'s face. They are not sure what is going on but they feel something. Their mouths get closer.*

They kiss.

Cut to CALUM *and* PRIEST.

PRIEST. What are you saying exactly? I don't appreciate being talked to like this when I've just found your daughter for you.

CALUM. You used to be a Priest.

PRIEST. That's no crime.

CALUM. I know a man just doesn't run away from everything to live in a shed hanging off the side of a cliff by himself. No woman. No job. No family around him. That man must be running away from something. A man would be suspicious about a man like that.

PRIEST. A man should keep his made up stories to himself.

CALUM. Aye. Well. (*Goes to head off.*) You take care now.

Back to ALEX *and* MARY. *They stop kissing.*

MARY. That was funny.

ALEX. Yeah . . .

Funny nice though.

MARY *nods.*

MARY. Dad'll be here soon.

ALEX. Will we wait for him?

MARY. No.

They leave. MARY *reaches over and holds* ALEX's *hand, gently, tentatively as they go off.*

Scene Nine

Back at home, in the main room. CATHERINE ANN *comes on with towels. Then* MARY *comes in, a bit wet. Looking miserable.*

CATHERINE ANN. We'll get these clothes off.

She pulls her jumper off over her head in that motherly way. MARY *is all arms, head stuck in neck of jumper. She starts drying her off and putting her clothes on the clothes horse.*

You're soaking. What you were thinking I don't know.

CALUM *comes on.*

CALUM. Make sure she's warm enough.

CATHERINE ANN. What do you think I'm doing.

CALUM. She looks cold.

CATHERINE ANN. Wouldn't you be more use in the other room.

CALUM. Um . . . right.

He leaves.

CATHERINE ANN. Your father was worried sick about you.

MARY. I know. I'm sorry. I wasn't really thinking.

CATHERINE ANN. He said that Priest found you.

MARY. Yes.

CATHERINE ANN. Was it the fire that scared you away?

MARY. Yes.

CATHERINE ANN. And Priest found you did he, not long before Calum turned up.

MARY. Not long.

CATHERINE ANN. You know, the moor's no place to be. Ten minutes in the mist and you don't know anything. And at night as well.

Are you warm enough?

MARY *nods.*

I'll leave you be to get changed.

CATHERINE ANN *leaves the room. MARY dries herself off with a towel. She isn't wearing much, we can see her shoulders and her back as she gets ready to change.*

MICHEAL *has come in and is watching her.*

She turns to pick up an item of clothing and sees him there.

MARY. Been there for a while, have you?

MICHEAL. No.

MARY. Well. Pass over my clothes.

MICHEAL *picks up a small pile of dry clothes and go over to her.*

Stands in front of her. MARY expects him to put it down and go away.

Well. Put them down and leave.

MICHEAL. Maybe I don't want to.

Pause.

I know what you've been up to.

MARY. What?

MICHEAL. You've been busy.

MARY. What are you talking about?

MICHEAL. I know you started the fire. And you'll be going to prison or worse if you don't do exactly what I say. From now on.

MARY. We didn't start the fire.

MICHEAL. Well . . . it's not what happened that counts. It's what people think happened.

He reaches over and touches her shoulder.

MARY. What are you doing. Micheal, don't.

MICHEAL. Shut up.

ALEX *comes in.*

ALEX. Get away from her.

MICHEAL *stops suddenly. Turns around.*

MICHEAL (*to* MARY). Tell him to leave, or you'll be in trouble.

ALEX. You're not telling anybody anything.

MICHEAL. I'll do what I want.

ALEX. No you won't. Now get the hell away from Mary. (*To* MARY.) Are you alright?

MARY *has got away from* MICHEAL. *She nods. She puts some clothes on quickly.*

MICHEAL. Myself and Mary were talking. Now go away.

ALEX. God sakes Micheal, after the night she's had.

MICHEAL. It was Mary who wanted to talk to me.

ALEX. I don't think so.

MARY. Alex, just leave it.

ALEX. What?

MARY. Just . . . both of you leave me alone. I want to get dressed.

ALEX. Alright. (*To* MICHEAL.) Come on.

MICHEAL. I'll move when I want to.

ALEX. You'll move now.

MICHEAL. What'll you do about it.

ALEX. I'll gut you like a fish and cut your balls off with a pair of blunt sheep shears.

MICHEAL. You don't scare me.

MARY. Micheal, do I have to spell it out. Leave me alone. I'm not in the mood.

MICHEAL. That's not what you were saying to Priest earlier I bet.

MARY. What are you talking about.

ALEX. You're upsetting her.

MICHEAL. Lucky he found you so easily.

ALEX. I've had enough.

MICHEAL. What are you go to do then, measan na croich. [*Bloody lapdog.*]

Pause.

ALEX. I'm going to teach you a lesson you won't forget in a hurry.

They circle round, ALEX *trying to get closer to* MICHEAL.

MICHEAL. Why don't you just go. Nobody wants you here. You're nothing but boarded-outs. Your real parents didn't want you. My parents are only doing it for the money.

ALEX. What money.

MICHEAL. They get money to keep you.

ALEX. That's a lie.

MICHEAL. It's true.

ALEX. Grab him.

They both grab him and after a struggle dangle him upside down.

Tie him up.

MARY *ties his legs up.*

MICHEAL. What are you doing?

ALEX *pushes him to the ground.*

ALEX. Shut up you chicken faced little cat hater. You'll never touch Mary again.

ALEX *gets another rope and ties a big bowline knot in it to form a noose. Then he tries to force the noose over* MICHEAL*'s head.*

MICHEAL. I was only messing about! I wasn't going to do anything!

ALEX *manages to get the noose around his head.* MARY *has run off, she comes back.*

MARY. I got some scones we can throw at him!

ALEX *has the rope around* MICHEAL*'s neck and is riding him like a donkey.*

ALEX. Measan! I'll give you measan.

MICHEAL *is desperately trying to get out of this. He is trying to kick at the two of them but* ALEX *has the better of him.*

MARY *grabs the scones and start throwing them at him.* MICHEAL *is going blue.*

You like that! What do you think of that now! You blackmailing duff-eating bastard!

CALUM *appears.*

CALUM. What the hell is going on here. (*Sees* MICHEAL.) An diabhal orms'! [*Jesus Christ!*]

Have you lost your minds!

ALEX *drops the rope.* MICHEAL *collapses and starts gasping like a fish.*

MARY. He's as blue as a turbot lying there gasping.

CALUM. Turbot! I'll turbot you both!

This has gone far enough.

Both of you get inside.

Catherine Ann, phone the doctor.

Goes to MICHEAL

Are you alright son?

Are you alright?

MICHEAL *tries to croak something out.* CATHERINE ANN *is there now, trying to help* MICHEAL.

ALEX. It's his fault. He was/

CALUM (*shouts*). / I'll kill you, you little bastard! (*To* MICHEAL.) Can you talk son? (*To* ALEX.) By the time I'm finished with you, you'll wish it had been around your neck instead. And your mother spent all day making those scones.

ALEX. I'm sorry.

CALUM. Sorry? I'm the one who's sorry, for ever letting you into this house. You've been nothing but trouble from the moment you stepped in the door. We treated you well and you've made a laughing stock of this family.

ALEX. But you didn't see what he was doing! He was upsetting Mary.

CALUM. Catherine Ann, get the belt.

(*To* ALEX.) Drop your trousers.

CATHERINE ANN. Calum, no.

CALUM. Get my belt. He needs to be taught a lesson.

CATHERINE ANN. No.

CALUM. You now as well! You'll do what I say! While all of you are in my house you'll do what I say. Now go and get my belt!

He pushes her, but he pushes her a bit too hard and she stumbles to the ground.

Catherine Ann . . . I'm sorry.

CATHERINE ANN *has picked herself up.*

CATHERINE ANN. Don't you lay one finger on my child again.

CALUM *backs off.*

CALUM (*to* ALEX). You. Pack your bags.

You're leaving for Glasgow tomorrow.

CALUM *stalks off.*

CATHERINE ANN. Come on Micheal. Let's have a look at you. What were you doing that upset them so much.

MICHEAL. I didn't do anything.

CATHERINE ANN. Hmm . . . Och you'll be alright. Let's get you inside.

ALEX *and* MARY *are left alone.*

MARY. Do you think he's serious? About you having to go.

ALEX. I think he might be.

MARY. But what'll you do?

ALEX. Don't know.

Pause.

I'm sorry for causing so much trouble.

MARY. I don't want you to go.

ALEX. I don't want to go without you.

They hold one another then they turn their backs on one another and part.

Scene Ten

ALEX *stands on one side of the stage.* MARY *at the other.*

ALEX. I was sent away to learn a trade.

MARY. I can't believe Alex has gone.

ALEX. I was going to be a butcher.

MARY. I'm missing him butterflies.

    MARY *leaves.*

ALEX. I would be a new upright standing member of the community. My sister was to be a tailor at home, but she kept sticking her needles in people.

Backwards ferry and then overtoppling houses and black dirt streets. Tenement framed sky and tram lined clouds. No Mary. As lonely as a tree.

Why am I missing that place.

He looks around.

I'd forgotten how busy it was here.

ALEX *is on a busy street in Glasgow.*

Glasgow was a dirty whore of a place. But the biggest whore of all . . . was Pig.

PIG *and* SHOOEY *come on stage.* PIG *is a butcher, carrying a cleaver. He promenades. He has a big red face and wears blood-stained overalls.*

SHOOEY *is another apprentice. Fairly shy, with a stutter. Glaswegian. Spiky hair.* ALEX *and* SHOOEY *stand like recruits in front of him.*

The Pig smelled. I could smell him from the other end of the street smelled of animal insides and shit and disinfectant and rubber gloves and blood.

I'll have to ask him if he's married.

PIG. Right you little bastards! Who's the biggest loon in this place. Who's the biggest maddie. Well I'll tell you you're all nothing but little piglets in this place now and if I hear a bleat out of you I'll cut your balls off with my tobacco knife and eat them like the Spaniards do with some garlic and onions. Lovely.

Do you know any Spaniards, boy.

ALEX. No.

PIG. Well, that's what they do.

So. You will do as I say. There will be no deviation. A butcher's life is a hard life. But it's a good one. For one, you get respect. Respect! You do what uncle Pig says and you'll be alright. Right you little fuckers. Just you remember who the king Pig is here. I decide what happens to you. If you live like a potato for the rest of your life or if you die. Or, if you get out. I'm the daddy.

(*To* ALEX.) Who's your daddy?

ALEX. You are Mr Pig.

PIG (*to* SHOOEY). And who's *your* daddy?

SHOOEY. Eh eh you are miss misster p puh peeg.

PIG. Shut up!

SHOOEY. Right.

PIG. We. Are special. As butchers we do very special things. Things which other people don't want to do, aren't brave enough to do. We are the strong ones. The providers. The givers and takers away of life.

PIG *throws* ALEX *the cleaver.*

Are you strong enough. You bloody little teuchtar.

A pig runs on stage.

Go on! We don't got all day!

ALEX. Here pig.

PIG. It's not a fucking cat! Come on man!

ALEX (*his face clouds over*). Let the dance begin!

He pulls out a red cape, and starts to promenade around the pig.

I am the chop maker. I am king pork. I am the top daddy of Pigville. And you, are a pig. On my patch. He was an ugly grippon, not even his pig mother would have liked his moo.

ALEX *runs after the pig and chases it off the stage. We hear a squeal.* ALEX *comes back in, covered in blood. He has the pig's head on a platter. He lays it at* PIG's *feet.*

PIG. Good. Now . . . to work!

ALEX. That was my life. Cutting up pigs all day. Red blood covered and sore trotters chop chop.

SHOOEY. Hey. Bog man.

No answer.

Hey! Bog man!

You gonna be long at Pig's? P p Pig's?

ALEX. Leave me alone.

SHOOEY. No offence eh but smell eh. No offence heh heh eh? Smell it myself smell of it myself. Been with Pig's for few year now. Aye.

ALEX. I said leave me alone.

SHOOEY. Aye. Right enuff.

Pause.

Do you like your acu acu accumodation nice one eh? Betcha never seen nothing like it before.

ALEX. I have.

SHOOEY. See told you. Tell you another thing a year of cutting up pigs you feel like one yourself. Start to smeel smeeell like hem. Sniff but. Chop bucket chop bucket.

Don't even like bacon, but. Don't even like bacon.

They go off.

Scene Eleven

MARY *moping around inside the house.* CALUM *comes in.*

CALUM. Have you fed the animals yet?

MARY. I'm not feeling very well.

CALUM. What's wrong with you?

MARY. I've been a little sick.

CALUM. Are you over it?

MARY. Aye.

CALUM. The animals are needing fed. Peats to do as well.

MARY. I'll do it soon.

CALUM. Alright.

> CALUM *leaves.* MARY *forces herself to get up and starts to make ready to go out and work.* PRIEST *appears in the door.* MARY *gets a surprise.*

MARY. Jesus, you nearly scared me half to death.

PRIEST. Alright to come in.

MARY. Aye.

PRIEST. Is Calum about?

MARY. He is. But you're fine to visit.

PRIEST. Just wanted to see how things were going.

MARY. I'm alright.

PRIEST. Heard from Alex?

MARY. Yeah.

PRIEST. You must be missing him.

MARY. I'm alright I said.

PRIEST. Are you busy?

MARY. Yeah.

Pause.

I've just got a lot of things running through my head.

PRIEST. What's bothering you.

MARY. Well.

Don't laugh.

PRIEST. Mary . . .

MARY. I've heard of a guy in Glasgow. He helps homers find
their real parents. He's helped quite a few people. I was
thinking of maybe . . . trying to get in touch with him.

PRIEST. Is this something you want to do. Have you thought
hard about it. You open these doors and you can never shut
them again.

MARY. I think I'm sure.

PRIEST. Are things OK here?

MARY. I just feel . . . it's a big part of me which has
disappeared, as if it never existed. Like there's a glass wall
between me and . . . you must feel it's important, do you?
Not knowing what I am, all I know is this place and I feel
as if I'm drowning sometimes or that part of me is getting
so faint that I can hardly see it any more and this might
help make sense of it to me. I don't want them to take me
back or anything like that, I just want to know that they . . .
exist . . . and that I exist and the person I am is the person
I should be and that I'm not just a mistake. That this isn't
all a huge mistake.

PRIEST. Mary, you're certainly not that.

MARY. I think I'll write to Alex and see what he thinks. See if
he wants to find his parents as well.

PRIEST. Just . . . think about it for a while.

MARY. I'd love to see him.

PRIEST. Why don't you go and visit him.

MARY. I don't have the fare.

Pause. PRIEST *takes out his wallet, places some money on the table. Enough to cover her trip.*

What's this?

PRIEST. It's a gift.

MARY. I can't take that.

PRIEST. You're going to take it.

MARY. I'd rather save up for it myself.

PRIEST. How quickly could you do that?

Pause.

MARY. It's a lot of money.

PRIEST. I have enough.

MARY. I don't know what to say. Are you sure?

PRIEST. Yes.

MARY. Thank you.

She tentatively takes it. Goes over and gives PRIEST *a hug. They part.*

CALUM *comes in.*

CALUM. Tha thu sin. [*There you are.*]

PRIEST. A Chalum.

CALUM (*to* MARY). Have you done the animals yet?

MARY. I was just going to.

PRIEST. It was my fault, keeping her back.

CALUM (*to* PRIEST). Can I help you at all?

PRIEST. I was just passing.

Pause.

CALUM. Eh . . . I wanted to say to you. The night of the fire. Well. Thanks for helping Mary. For finding her.

PRIEST. 'Se do bheatha. No worries.

CALUM *nods.*

Better get on then. Take care, Mary. Tell Alex I was asking after him.

MARY. I promise I'll visit you soon . . .

PRIEST *goes.* CALUM *clears his throat.*

CALUM. Em . . . you'll notice more and more . . . men . . . will take an interest in you, you're at that age.

He is a bit embarrassed.

And. You can . . . see the birds. See the bees.

MARY. See the bees?

CALUM. You have to be careful now of the birds. And the bees.

MARY. I don't understand.

CALUM. Men like women. In a special way.

When a man likes a woman he gets big. Bigger. And he wants a lady to notice.

MARY. Big?

CALUM. And a lady has times. She has times in a month. *a* time.

MARY. Um . . .

CALUM. Oh . . . ask Catherine Ann.

Go on now, go on and do your work.

CALUM *leaves.* MARY *cannot help a wee smile.*

Before she goes out she gets a bit of paper, an envelope and a pen, and takes them with her.

Scene Twelve

Back in PIG*'s shop.* ALEX *and* SHOOEY *sitting around not working. A letter is thrown onto the stage at him.* ALEX *picks it up.*

ALEX. It's for me!

From Mary . . . Shooey it's from Mary.

SHOOEY. Nice wan man.

ALEX *tears it open excitedly and reads it.*

ALEX. She says she's coming down.

He reads on some more. His face gets serious. PIG *comes on.*

PIG. Sitting around! Am ah running a sitting around shop?

SHOOEY. No Mr Pig.

PIG. Start chopping then!

They get up and start chopping.

Chop for your lives you little teuchtar bastards.

SHOOEY. Ah'm no a teuchtar Mr Pig.

PIG. You're as bad as any teuchtar you glaickit wee excuse of a flatfish of a man.

ALEX. I'm not a teuchtar either.

PIG. Shut up! Did I say I had stopped talking! I'll make a teuchtar flavoured casserole of both of you like a mad fucking teuchtar eating casserole making frenchman so get on with it.

PIG *leaves.* ALEX *and* SHOOEY *working as hard as they can.* ALEX *cuts in the wrong place and a burst of blood sprays his face. He stops working.*

ALEX. I hate this place.

I hate this place.

I . . . hate . . . this . . . place . . .

And then starts the pig dance. The pigs come on and dance around him with SHOOEY. ALEX *finally cracks.*

Noooooo!!!

The pigs dance off. Mr PIG *comes on.*

PIG. Am ah a parrot! How many times do I have to say the same hing you pair of chicken arse shit handed excuses. Clean up that mess.

ALEX. All of my life I've had people telling me what to do. And if I didn't do it and if I didn't want to do it – it was I got hell. Until one day you feel something snap inside you and you think – hell, why should I. And that's what happened with Mr Pig.

PIG. Clean up that mess.

ALEX. I looked at myself, covered in pigshit and pig guts everywhere and something snapped.

Do it yourself you fucking fat, red piece of MANYURE.

The Pig pricked up his piggy ears.

PIG. What? What did I hear you say?

ALEX. Pick up your own shit you pig shit smelling bastard.

PIG *picks up a cleaver. There is a table in the middle of the floor.*

PIG. You little shit. I take you in and this is what I get from you. I've had boys like you before think they're the bee's fucking knees all tough with their cutting up dead animals, few weeks of it they think they can take on the Pig, think they be as big as a cow's bladder well I'll tell you, you little shit you'll pick up your shovel AND you'll shovel THOSE pig insides until I tell you to stop and if you don't I'll cut you into little cubes so that you'll be too small to make a pot of mince out of how does that sound you bloody little heathen.

ALEX. Away and fuck yourself.

Pause.

PIG. Oh aye. It's like that, is it.

The PIG *grabs him and throws* ALEX *down on the table on top of the chops. He holds the cleaver in the air.*

I'll chop you up into little pieces. You've the cheek of a donkey. What'll your mother think of that! You know where the last boy said something like that to me ended up – wrapped up in bloody paper and looking out the front window of the shop along with all the other pigs with no manners.

SHOOEY, *who has been standing at the side, suddenly cracks.*

SHOOEY. Leave him alone!

He grabs a pig's head and hits PIG *with it.* PIG *rolls off* ALEX.

Why you bah bah don't treat people nice! Why you no treat people a little bit nuh . . . nuh . . . NICE!

PIG (*gets up, cleaver in hand*). You just get back to your pigs and we'll forget about this little incident. I just want a quick word with Alex.

SHOOEY *runs at him, pighead in hand and launches himself at him. He brings the pighead down on him so that* PIG'*s head is stuffed inside it. It is like he is wearing a big pig helmet.* PIG *can't see anything and staggers about.*

SHOOEY *has a bucket and he is hitting* PIG *with it.*

SHOOEY. Five years eh not a p p pound to mah name you treat me like a nyi a nyi A NYIDIOT! Shooey dae this Shooey dae that AHV HAD ENUFF!

SHOOEY *grabs the cleaver and drags* PIG *offstage.* ALEX *is left on stage. He winces with each blow that* SHOOEY *delivers.*

Then silence.

ALEX. Oh dear.

Oh dear oh dear oh dear.

SHOOEY *comes back in.*

SHOOEY (*in a high-pitched voice*). Oh dear.

What have I done!

ALEX. I don't know. I don't know.

SHOOEY. Whit! Whit!

ALEX. Shut up!

SHOOEY. What! What! Bih . . . durrr . . . .bih . . . durr . . .
This is . . . what!

ALEX. We'll not tell anyone.

SHOOEY. You're right! That'll be our plan.

ALEX. Nobody.

SHOOEY. No-one!

ALEX. Business as usual.

SHOOEY. Of course!

ALEX. Get rid of him then.

SHOOEY. Eh? I already did.

ALEX. Get rid of the body.

SHOOEY. Well, a wee huh huh hand like.

ALEX. Well, I didn't do it.

SHOOEY. Credit due credit due . . . stepped into a nasty shityu
situation saving your bacon like.

ALEX. I didn't ask you to kill him!

SHOOEY. Help us dig a hole anyway man.

ALEX. Just go and sort it out!

SHOOEY. Right. Right enuff.

ALEX. And that was that as they say in the Gaelic. At least we didn't have to listen to Pig anymore. And Shooey was happy because the shock cured his stutter.

SHOOEY. A peck of pickled peppers peter piper picked she sells sea shells by the sea shore red leather yellow leather . . .

SHOOEY goes off. Pause.

ALEX. I want to go home.

SHOOEY runs back on with a trolley – SHOOEY grabs the edge of the sheet and pulls it off. It is covered in juicy cuts of PIG.

SHOOEY. Ladies! Gentlemen! Get your finest Pig here! Grade A top notch home grown corn fed juicy juicy Pig.

An imaginary crowd gathers.

Good evening ladies.

Ladies and Gentlemen: Good evening. Get your quality Pig here. Guarantees! Guarantees you won't eat anything like it. Thank you. Thank you . . . Do come again . . .

A hit.

A palpable hit with the proles.

ALEX. What are you doing!

SHOOEY. Eh?

ALEX. That's not . . .

SHOOEY. Got to earn some money man some bread spondulicks but. You told me to eh eh get rid of him like.

ALEX. Shooey, Mary's supposed to be arriving soon. We can't have the place looking like an abattoir.

SHOOEY. That's funny man! . . . this IS an abattoir! Sort of like wan. An abattoir for pigs but!

ALEX. Shooey. Go out the back and wash the chickens.

SHOOEY. Eh. Right enuff.

SHOOEY *leaves.* ALEX *sits down. Takes out* MARY's *letter. It is a bit bloody. Reads a little of it. Then with a new purpose he gets up. Takes off his bloody clothes and puts on good clothes.*

MARY *is due to arrive soon. He gets himself ready and waits. He looks at his watch.*

However, it is the postman again.

POSTMAN. Letter for MacNeil.

ALEX. That's me.

It's from Mary.

This is unexpected. He opens it quickly and reads it.

I've got to . . . got to go . . . . Shooey!

Shoeey runs in.

SHOOEY. Yes sur?

ALEX. You hold the fort. I've got to go home.

SHOOEY. Eh . . . like hame did you forget something hame?

ALEX. Home home, Shooey. Home home.

SHOOEY. Right. Teuchtars! Up there like. No problem ahm in control.

ALEX. And so for the second time I found myself on the ferry slicing through the black mirror of the sea and making my way to the island.

Scene Thirteen

MARY *is at home in the kitchen. She is working.* PRIEST *comes in.*

PRIEST. Hi there.

MARY. Hi.

PRIEST. Are you busy?

MARY. Usual.

PRIEST. So you're heading off soon.

MARY. I wanted to talk to you about that. I'm not going now.

She takes out the money he had given her previously.

I wanted to give you this back.

PRIEST. I don't want it. It was a present.

MARY. But I'm not going to Glasgow.

PRIEST. I don't care how you spend it.

MARY. Really. I'd rather

PRIEST. I was thinking, we haven't been to see a film for a while. Maybe you'd fancy.

MARY. Maybe. Maybe in a while. I'll think about it.

Pause.

PRIEST. Hear anything from Alex?

MARY. He writes quite a lot.

Pause.

PRIEST. It's a bit lonely you know, living up near the cliffs. And I was thinking. Well, I've got a bit of money. So I was thinking of maybe moving. Getting a house somewhere in the village. There'd be plenty of rooms there.

MARY. Sounds nice.

PRIEST. Well, I was thinking if you'd like to move in. There'd be plenty of room.

MARY. I don't have any money to pay you for the room.

PRIEST. You wouldn't have to pay me. I'd take care of you.

Pause.

I think we'd be good for each other.

You're old enough now, to decide what you want to do yourself. Your parents couldn't stop you.

And you said you wanted to leave here.

Will you think of . . . my offer at least.

MARY. I can't.

I think you should go. My father'll be back soon.

PRIEST. Will you at least . . . think of what I've said.

MARY. You don't understand. I can't. Go. Please go.

PRIEST, *resigned, goes.* MARY *slumps in a chair.*

ALEX *is home. He stands in the doorway surveying the room.* MARY *thinks it's* PRIEST *coming back . . . But she turns and sees* ALEX. *There is a momentary pause as she takes it in. Then she rushes over to him.*

Alex!

ALEX *drops his bag and they embrace.*

ALEX. Bha mi worried ma do dheidhinn. [*I was worried about you.*]

MARY. Bha mi gad ionndrainn. [*I missed you.*]

ALEX. I missed you too.

How have you been keeping?

MARY. Oh . . . alright.

Pause.

Did you get my letter?

ALEX. Yes.

ALEX. You shouldn't have told me in a letter.

MARY. I didn't know what to do.

ALEX. Are you sure?

MARY. Yes.

ALEX. Is that why you didn't come to Glasgow?

MARY. I guess. I needed some time to think abut what to do.

ALEX. You're sure it's me.

MARY. Who else do you think it would be.

He takes it in.

ALEX. I didn't think it could happen on the first time.

MARY. Either did I.

ALEX. You're not showing yet.

MARY. No.

Alex, what are we going to do.

Silence.

ALEX. I don't . . . I don't know.

MARY. Neither do I.

ALEX. You know, I heard of some doctors in Glasgow . . . that can help.

MARY. What do you mean?

ALEX. It would mean you wouldn't have to have it.

MARY. Alex, we're Catholic.

ALEX. Jesus Jesus . . . stupid . . . how could we be so stupid . . . I'm sorry Mary. I'm so sorry.

MARY. It's my fault as much as yours. We just got carried away. You leaving and everything.

Pause.

Supposed to be family. What'll everyone think?

ALEX. I don't care.

ALEX *is thinking.*

Well we've not let each other down before.

I'll stay with you. Whatever you want to do.

She goes over to him and gives him a hug. They hold each other tightly.

Have you told them?

MARY. No.

ALEX. Maybe we can go to Glasgow. We can just leave. Now.

MARY. We can't just do that. Imagine how hurt mam would be.

ALEX *thinks.*

ALEX. I've got enough money to set us up here.

MARY. We don't have to tell anyone it was . . . you . . . I mean us.

ALEX. Who will you say it was?

MARY. I don't have to say it was anyone.

ALEX. You'll keep the place in gossip for the next twenty years.

MARY. To hell with the lot of them.

ALEX. You'll have to tell mam and dad sometime.

MARY. I guess.

So you'll . . . we'll be alright.

ALEX. We'll be fine.

At that moment the door opens. CALUM *comes in.*

He is still for a moment, surprised that ALEX *is there.* ALEX *and* MARY *stop their conversation straight away.* CATHERINE ANN *comes in and sees him.*

CATHERINE ANN. Alex!

ALEX. Hello mam.

She gives him a hug.

CATHERINE ANN. But you didn't say you were coming. What a surprise!

ALEX. It was a spur of the moment thing.

CATHERINE ANN. How was your crossing?

ALEX. Fine. Flat as a mirror.

He turns to face CALUM. *They nod at one another.*

CALUM. Alex.

CALUM *sits.*

(*To* CATHERINE ANN.) Make me a cup of tea, would you.

CATHERINE ANN. Yes. A cup of tea.

MARY. Are you OK mam? Did Micheal get away OK?

CATHERINE ANN. Yes. (*To* ALEX.) Micheal's gone off to join the Merchant Navy.

ALEX. That's good.

CATHERINE ANN. What a lovely surprise! Tell me all about Glasgow.

ALEX. Glasgow's alright. I'm a butcher now.

CATHERINE ANN. I wish you'd told me you were coming, I'd have made up the room for you.

ALEX. It's fine, mam.

CATHERINE ANN. How long will you be staying?

ALEX. I was thinking of staying for a while.

CATHERINE ANN. Really?

ALEX. I've saved up a little money. Might be enough to buy a share on a boat.

CATHERINE ANN. Sounds like your boss was good to you.

ALEX. Looks like it.

CALUM. Mary, get me the sugar will you.

MARY *obediently gets up.*

CATHERINE ANN. I think Mary's a bit bored staying at home while you're off gallivanting in the big city. Nothing really happens here, eh Mary.

MARY. Aye.

Pause.

ALEX. I think once I get a place to stay Mary's moving in with me.

CATHERINE ANN. Oh? (*To* MARY.) You never mentioned any of this.

MARY. I'd no plans till now.

CATHERINE ANN. But you've no job.

ALEX. I've enough saved.

CATHERINE ANN. There's plenty space here, both of you can stay here for/ . . .

MARY. Mam, I'm pregnant.

CATHERINE ANN. /the . . . time . . . being.

CALUM. You're what?

CATHERINE ANN. But . . . Are you sure . . .

MARY *nods.*

Why didn't you tell me?

MARY. I was scared.

CATHERINE ANN. I'm not sure . . . this is a lot to take in. Well . . . how long gone are you?

MARY. About three months. (MARY *is starting to get upset.*)

CATHERINE ANN. Ssshhh now.

CALUM. Who's the father?

CATHERINE ANN. Leave the girl alone. She's upset.

CALUM. I'm asking her a question.

CATHERINE ANN. Leave the girl alone!

CALUM. She's old enough to answer for herself! What the
hell were you thinking, eh? Well, I'm not going to have this
family a laughing stock. Who did it? Was it that Priest
fellow? He's been sniffing around you like a dog couldn't
you have kept yourself under control oinseach na croich.
[*Stupid bitch.*]

CATHERINE ANN. I won't have you talking to her like that.

CALUM. Shut up Catherine Ann. I'll show that bastard what
happens when he takes advantage of young girls.

MARY. It wasn't him.

CALUM. Coming to my house. My house! Making a fool of
me under my own roof!

CATHERINE ANN. Calm down.

CALUM. Calm down! What do you suggest we do then!

CATHERINE ANN. Do we know the father?

CALUM. Of course we know the father.

MARY *is quiet.*

CATHERINE ANN. Mary can have it, and we can say that it's
mine. I know someone who's done that.

CALUM. Exactly. You know about them. You'd never be able
to keep it quiet. What do we do when she starts showing.

CATHERINE ANN. Maybe she can go to Glasgow with Alex.

CALUM. You're too old to have another child.

CATHERINE ANN. I am not. Plenty of women have had
children at my age.

CALUM. But you can't *have* a child.

CATHERINE ANN. Oh for God's sake! That doesn't matter!

CALUM. But people know you can't have another one.

CATHERINE ANN. What does it matter what people think! These are our children.

CALUM. They have nothing to do with us.

CATHERINE ANN. Oh you were always a selfish man, but this . . . You can't even think of ways to try and help them.

CALUM (*losing his temper*). This is all your fault. Sneaking around with that Priest, didn't we say he was no good. But you would never listen to us. You've done nothing but disobey me both of you since you stepped in the door. I take you into my home and all you do is lie to me. I'll have no more of it, you hear, no more of it!

ALEX. Leave her alone.

They face each other.

CALUM. Get out of my house.

ALEX. I did it.

Pause.

CALUM. What.

CATHERINE ANN. What are you talking about Alex.

ALEX. It was me.

CALUM. If this is one of your jokes . . .

ALEX. It's the truth.

CALUM. Your sister.

ALEX. Not by birth.

CALUM. You little bastard . . . salachair an diobhal coming into my house . . . [*Dirty bastard coming into my house.*]

ALEX. We've only ever had each other. You've treated me worse than a dog, and she's nothing more than a slave to you and your bloody hypocritical god fearing wouldn't even stretch to treating us both with a little kindness.

CALUM. Kindness! What would you know of kindness and the work your mother and I have done to make sure both of you are looked after.

CATHERINE ANN. Calm down . . . you're making her even more upset . . .

CALUM. We take you in and this is how you repay us. You know what people will say about this? You know what people will say about me?

ALEX. A laughing stock, eh.

CALUM cracks. He grabs ALEX by the throat and pushes him down on a table.

CALUM. I've had enough of you – you'll wish you never set foot inside this house when I'm done with you. I'll kill you.

He has ALEX by the throat.

MARY. Leave him alone.

(*Louder.*) Let him go!

It is the mother who cracks. CALUM has almost got the better of ALEX, when totally unexpectedly CATHERINE ANN slaps CALUM hard in the face.

CATHERINE ANN. That's enough.

CALUM lets ALEX go and reels back.

(*Quieter.*) That's enough.

CALUM. Catherine Ann . . .

CATHERINE ANN. Don't you go near my children again.

CALUM. But . . .

CATHERINE ANN. Just go.

CALUM is rooted to the spot.

CALUM. You put them before me.

CATHERINE ANN. I don't want you here. Any more. Just go.

CALUM looks around, and leaves.

A long pause.

MARY. Should I go after him.

CATHERINE ANN. No.

MARY. He'll be back though.

CATHERINE ANN. I don't know a ghraidh. I don't know.

CATHERINE ANN *tries to regain her strength.*

MARY. I've made such a mess of everything.

CATHERINE ANN. You'll be fine.

CATHERINE ANN *is beside her, comforting her, stroking her hair.*

Bidh thu slàn mas pòs thu. You'll be whole before you marry.

MARY *smiles. She has stopped crying.*

MARY. Tha mi'n dòchas. I hope so.

They both smile at this.

CATHERINE ANN. Nach eil fhios agad gum bi. Of course you will be.

You know you will be.

CATHERINE ANN *tries to quietly re-assert some normality after the argument. As the lights go down, a simple domestic scene.*

Alex, suidh sios. Sit . . . you'll be tired. Bidh thu sgìth as deidh an trip agad. [*Alex, sit down. You'll be tired after your trip.*]

ALEX. Tha mi alright. [*I'm alright.*]

CATHERINE ANN. Thalla's suidh comhla ri Mairi. [*Go and sit with Mary.*]

ALEX *goes to sit beside* MARY *as* CATHERINE ANN *makes herself busy in the kitchen. They talk quietly and normally, back and forth now and again in Gaelic.*

Bha mi dol a dheanamh cupan teatha. [*I was going to make a cup of tea.*]

MARY. Nì mis' e. [*I'll give you a hand.*]

CATHERINE ANN. Fuirich thus' an-sin. It's no bother. [*You stay there. It's no bother.*]

Pause.

Bheil an t-acras oirbh? [*Are you both hungry?*]

ALEX. Rud beag. [*A bit.*]

Pause.

CATHERINE ANN (*to* MARY). Na chuir thu an ròsd dhan àbhainn? [*Did you put that roast in the oven?*]

MARY. Chuir. Cha bhith e fada. [*I did. It shouldn't be long.*]

Pause.

CATHERINE ANN. De seòrsa biadh a bhiodh thu dèanamh dhut fhèin ann an Glaschu co-dhiù? [*What kind of food did you make for yourself in Glasgow anyway?*]

ALEX. Tòrr rudan. Tòrr rudan. [*Lots of things. Lots of things.*]

Just before it goes to black MARY *reaches over and touches* ALEX's *hand. He holds hers.*

Black.

A Nick Hern Book

Homers first published in Great Britain in 2002
as a paperback original by Nick Hern Books Limited,
14 Larden Road, London W3 7ST, in association with
the Traverse Theatre, Edinburgh

Homers copyright © 2002 Iain F MacLeod

Iain F MacLeod has asserted her right to be identified
as the author of this work

Typeset by Country Setting, Kingsdown, Kent CT14 8ES
Printed and bound in Great Britain by Biddles, Guildford

ISBN 1 85459 727 2

A CIP catalogue record for this book is available from
the British Library